COMPETITIVE INTERFERENCE AND
TWENTIETH CENTURY DIPLOMACY

COMPETITIVE INTERFERENCE AND TWENTIETH CENTURY DIPLOMACY

RICHARD W. COTTAM

University of Pittsburgh Press

To the Memory
of my
Mother

ACKNOWLEDGMENTS

As MY former students will recognize, most of the ideas in this book were developed in my classes in international relations. It is to these students that I must acknowledge my primary debt. Their criticisms and comments compelled me to clarify my thinking and helped me avoid many an analytical dead end. In particular I owe much to Miss Gerry Sack for her sharp criticisms and her encouragement. Peter Galie and John Wolff were my research assistants.

My colleagues at the University of Pittsburgh were most helpful. Two of them, Holbert Carroll and Richard Park, read the manuscript in its entirety. William Polk of the University of Chicago commented extensively on the manuscript and made many valuable suggestions.

CONTENTS

INTRODUCTION

HAS AMERICAN diplomacy kept abreast of the revolutionary changes in technology and world politics? The huge building complex that houses the Department of State would seem to symbolize an affirmative answer to this perennial question. Compared to its meager pre-World War II predecessor, the new Department of State edifice reflects accurately the change in American diplomatic responsibilities. Furthermore, working within this building and in the scores of embassies around the world are men of unquestioned competence and steadily growing expertise.

But the response to the challenge to western leadership in terms of manpower and physical plant is the easy part. More difficult is the question of whether the style of diplomacy also has accommodated itself to the technological revolution and the spreading of political awareness to every corner of the earth, or whether the American style of diplomacy remains an essentially ad hoc one in which diplomats deal intuitively and individually with each succeeding crisis. The surface answer to this question seems to be that the style has indeed changed. Vast bureaucracies have today replaced the handful of diplomats of a half century ago. This implies acceptance of the conclusion that a style of diplomacy which was suitable for the eighteenth and nineteenth centuries, when aristocratic elites presided over a politically inert mass, is hopelessly inadequate in this era of mass awakening. Now the diplomatic community must concern itself with great socio-political movements rather than with the whims of a king or the intrigues of a traditional oligarchy. Today it is implicitly recognized that the diplomat, brilliant though he may be, cannot have the competence to handle individually a major diplomatic problem.

The ad hoc style of diplomacy has of course been inadequate for generations, and in the interwar period grossly so. Confronted with accelerating trends toward fascism, American as well as British and French diplomacy did virtually nothing to halt or redirect them. Since World War II the American people have accepted the necessity for large-scale American governmental involvement in an effort to contain and, if possible, reverse trends that are favorable to an expansion of communism. This change in attitude has made possible the spectacular growth in the size of the American foreign policy bureaucratic community and the growth of American involvement in the internal affairs of virtually every noncommunist state. Yet, for all that, the argument is a strong one that basically the American diplomatic style remains ad hoc and that both the general strategic policy of containment and more specific strategies such as the Alliance for Progress are essentially policy umbrellas for a series of ad hoc responses to local challenges.

The Suez crisis of 1956 illustrates this point. In the struggle to contain communism the Arab Middle East could hardly avoid becoming a major battlefield. Its strategic location and its role as the major supplier of oil for western Europe's industries assured a western resolve to keep it out of communist hands. At the same time Arab society and politics had reached a stage of development at which political convulsions were probable. Furthermore these convulsions were likely to redound to the advantage of the Soviet Union. Many Arabs, particularly young, educated ones, perceived as their central task the replacement of a traditionalist elite which had long collaborated with western imperialism. In the minds of these young men rapid social and economic progress, similar to that which had taken place in the Soviet Union, was called for. Though only a minority of this group was communist, most accepted the conclusion that only central governmental control and planning could produce the necessary transformation. Almost all believed passionately in Arab unity and the need ultimately to establish a great Arab state. Then, in cacophonous counterpoint to the major theme, sounds of the Arab-Israeli dispute arose. This also was to the Soviets' advantage. Arabs generally and the young modernists in particular viewed the state of Israel as a western creation established as part of an imperialist scheme to keep the Arab Middle East a weak semi-colony producing only raw materials.

Yet the West was not without assets in the eyes of this modernist group. Many of them had been educated in western institutions either abroad or in the Middle East. Of these a consistently underestimated number emerged with a devotion to free institutions. In fact as a group they were probably philosophically closer to the West than were the traditional leaders with whom western diplomats appeared to be more comfortable. Furthermore their nationalism was genuine and, except for the communist minority, they had no desire to substitute Soviet for western domination.

The central problem for American diplomacy in this era in the Middle East, therefore, was how to deal with Arab nationalism. The critical question that needed to be asked was: "Is the sociopolitical trend in the Arab states likely to result in a modernist-nationalist victory in the immediate future; and, if so, does American diplomacy have the capability for influencing the leadership and ideological focus of that movement in such a way as to reduce its attraction to the Soviet Union and to encourage an accommodation with Israel?" To answer such a question even tentatively required that a very careful and operationally focused analysis of the situation be made by men with an intimate understanding of each of the actors. Despite American newness in the Middle East, men with this competence were to be found in the State Department in 1956. But such a question would be asked only if policy formulation was long-term rather than ad hoc in focus; the course of events indicated that the question was never asked.

In 1956 the Arab nationalist modernizers had in President Gamal Abdul Nasser a hero and a leader who symbolized their struggle for national dignity and rapid modernization. American relations with the Nasser regime from the July, 1952, coup until the withdrawal in 1956 of the offer to finance the Aswan Dam were cordial and at times even affectionate. Even the shock of the Soviet-Czechoslovakian arms agreement with Egypt in 1955, though serious, was not great enough to destroy this pattern. Were one to look only at American-Egyptian relations, the answer to the basic question stated above would appear to be: "Yes; and the United States has the ability to guide the nationalist movement by a close working relationship with Gamal Abdul Nasser." At least Anthony Eden thought this was the answer (and the wrong answer) to the question.[1]

There was at the same time an Arab leader who symbolized to an equal degree the pro-British traditional elements—Nuri as-Said of Iraq. American support for the Iraqi regime that Nuri as-Said dominated was nothing short of enthusiastic up to the day in July, 1958, when that regime was overthrown and Nuri as-Said was murdered.[2] American policy here would argue that the answer to

1. Anthony Eden, *Full Circle* (Boston, Mass., 1960), pp. 248–90.
2. For clear evidence that American support for Nuri as-Said sometimes became, for individual American diplomats, adulation see Waldemar J. Gallman, *Iraq Under General Nuri* (Baltimore, Md., 1964).

the question was: "No; and the United States has the ability to guide the traditional Arab elite along a path toward modernization and a broadened base of support." But there is every reason to believe this critical question was never asked.

A much more reasonable conclusion would be that American policies in Egypt and Iraq were not coordinated through any long-term strategy and that each was an ad hoc response to a specific situation. To achieve the central goal of political stability under noncommunist leaders, the United States supported a strong modernist leader in one state, a traditionalist in the other. Implicit in these two policies were opposite assumptions regarding the long-term trend of Arabs politics.

Despite the denials of John Foster Dulles,[3] there is little reason to doubt Eden's conclusion that it was Dulles who precipitated the Suez crisis with his abrupt cancellation of the offer to finance the construction of the Aswan Dam.[4] From this action it is easy to infer an answer to the question posed above. Bringing the Middle East with its countless conflicts and subconflicts into crisis was an audacious act to say the very least. If it is assumed that the government had a full awareness of the situation, such a policy implies a conclusion that the trend of events was so unfavorable that only the strongest action could bring about a reversal. The inferred answer to the above question would therefore be: "Yes, an Arab nationalist victory is likely and is almost certain to be beyond our ability to control. Only the most determined action can prevent such a

3. Mr. Dulles' biographers either implicitly or explicitly accept responsibility for Dulles. Drummond and Coblentz contend that Eden must share the responsibility (Roscoe Drummond and Gaston Coblentz, *Duel at the Brink* [Garden City, N. Y., 1960] p. 170). See also John Ransom Beal, *John Foster Dulles: A Biography* (New York, 1957); Mildred H. Comfort, *John Foster Dulles, Peacemaker* (Minneapolis, 1960); Richard J. M. Goold-Adams, *The Time of Power: A Reappraisal of John Foster Dulles* (London, 1962); Deane and David Heller, *John Foster Dulles: Soldier for Peace* (New York, 1960). For a most explicit assertion of Dulles' responsibility see Herman Finer, *Dulles Over Suez* (Chicago, 1964).

4. Eden, *Full Circle*, pp. 485–86.

victory, which would do serious damage to our primary interests in the area." Since American primary interest was to contain the Soviet Union, the further conclusion can be drawn that the trend of Arab nationalism was favorable to the Soviets. Little wonder that throughout the Middle East the American cancellation was assumed to be a prelude to an American-backed effort to overturn the Nasser regime.

But the fears of some Arab leaders and the hopes of others that the withdrawal of the offer to finance the Aswan Dam was a prelude to a full-scale assault on a Nasser-focused Arab nationalism were not to materialize. In the months following Nasser's angry retaliatory action in nationalizing the Suez Canal, the Dulles policy was one of trying to restore the status quo ante. A far more reasonable explanation of the American action was that Dulles was exasperated by Nasser's negotiating with the Soviets, asserting his place among the neutralist Big Three, and above all daring to recognize Red China.[5] Dulles had been under strong pressure from Congress to take a hard line with Nasser and there was little enthusiasm for American financing of the Aswan Dam. Since Nasser added almost daily to the difficulty Dulles had in maintaining cordial relationships, Dulles could hardly be blamed for becoming annoyed. His cancellation of the financial proposal was therefore probably in part an angry impulse; the crisis that followed was not anticipated.

In the four-month period between nationalization of the Suez Canal Company and the launching of the Israeli invasion of Sinai, American policy did give evidence for the first time of a central focus on Arab nationalism. The inferred answer to the question at this point could be: "Yes, the victory of Arab nationalism under Nasser's leadership is inevitable, and to restrain it from passing over to the Soviet side we must accept the risk of breaking temporarily with our two closest allies." Such an inference is reasonable since there were alternative leaders to Nasser in the Arab world

5. Beal, *Dulles: A Biography*, p. 257; Finer, *Dulles Over Suez*, pp. 42–45.

who would have welcomed the overthrow of Nasser and his replacement by a more traditional figure. President Chamoun of Lebanon and Nuri as-Said of Iraq, despite their public remarks, were privately dismayed at the American reaction to the nationalization of the canal company; and these two gentlemen had been the closest friends of American policy in the Arab world. Therefore, the American action seems to imply a conclusion that an Egyptian Nuri as-Said could not control his country.

It is possible to believe that in this stage of the Suez crisis American foreign policy analysts differed profoundly from the British and French in their estimates of the meaning of Arab nationalism and that this difference was primarily responsible for the disunity among the allies in October, 1956. But it should be remembered that the Suez crisis was a compound of a bewildering number of lesser conflicts of great diversity, each interacting with the other. Each actor perceived the situation differently and responded with strategies that reflected confusion and internal disagreement.[6] The Soviet Union was seeking to establish itself as the disinterested friend of Arab nationalism while simultaneously encouraging the growth of communist parties or underground movements, which Arab nationalists understood would subvert nationalist purposes. Great Britain had reluctantly withdrawn her troops from the Suez Canal but her diplomatic activity in support of traditional Arab leaders left little doubt in Arab minds that she intended to retain a semicolonial hold on the area.[7] France, angry at being excluded from the Baghdad Pact, accused the British of failing to understand the significance of Arab nationalism but, because of the aid President Nasser had given to the Algerian rebels, she was looking for the opportunity to destroy the symbolic leader of Arab nationalism.[8]

6. For a description of the varied perceptions of the participants see Ismail Sabri Makled, "Comparative International Behavior in the Suez Crisis: A Perspective Study," Ph.D. diss., University of Pittsburgh, 1964.

7. *Ibid.*, pp. 56–63.

8. *Ibid.*, pp. 219–26, 229–36.

Israel, deeply divided in popular attitudes regarding the best way of dealing with the Arab foe, had turned to the leadership of a belligerent Ben Gurion. The Arabs, caught up in the Cold War, an anticolonial struggle, and bitter conflict with Israel, were themselves hopelessly divided. Traditionalist leaders, who controlled most of the Arab states, fought the modernist onslaught, often with great skill; but the traditional Saudi leaders preferred an alliance with the modernist Nasser to one with their hated rivals, the traditionalist Hashemite family of Iraq and Jordan; and under the surface of the modernist national movement competing leadership groups were forming and waiting for the struggle for control of that movement.

The role played by the United States in the crisis following the Suez invasion by Israel had an impact on Arab nationalism that might have been anticipated. The rapidly evolving image of a United States as the fourth in a partnership with British colonialism, Zionism, and traditional Arab leadership was seriously blurred. Among pro-Nasser forces throughout the Middle East, the United States and the Soviet Union shared a top popularity billing. From this point of view alone the American policy could be judged a spectacular success. Four months earlier Dulles had precipitated the crisis and in so doing had become the arch villain for Nasserites. The potential for a Soviet monopoly as the great power advocate of Arab modernist-nationalists was sharply reduced, although it should be noted that the inglorious Soviet role in suppressing the Hungarian revolt occurred simultaneously with the Suez invasion and this helped reduce the attractiveness of Soviet offers of support.

But the price paid for these gains was extraordinarily heavy. The strategic importance of the Arab Middle East was, after all, largely a result of the most central aspect of the containment policy, i.e., the defense of western Europe; therefore, to damage the western alliance in order to gain a problematic advantage in the Middle East was to permit ancillary aspects to dominate general policy.

Obviously the top priority objective in the months that followed had to be to repair the western alliance. But it does not follow that a change in policy in the Middle East was necessary for that rapprochement. On the contrary, the course of events in the Suez crisis provided circumstantial evidence that the American estimate of the strength of pro-Nasser Arab nationalists was correct and that the British and French estimate was incorrect. And indeed, when the American policy pronouncement on the Middle East was made, it was not at all clear that policy had changed. At first the Eisenhower Doctrine with its built-in ambiguities was more intriguing than dismaying for the Nasserites. But by the spring of 1957 the meaning of that doctrine was clear—it was a vehicle to isolate Nasser and to destroy his influence in the Arab world.

Why this alteration in policy occurred can only be a matter of speculation, but two factors are clear. First, the United States was anxious to accommodate British and French attitudes in the Middle East and these attitudes were intensely anti-Nasser. Second, the actions and attitudes of two Arab kings permitted a reappraisal of Nasser's potential. King Saud in early 1957 made clear his determination to resist any further advance of the pro-Nasser forces. He was even willing to put aside his hereditary conflict with the Hashemite family of Jordan and Iraq and to join forces with this family in combating Nasser. At the same time, King Hossein of Jordan, who had temporarily sided with Nasser and who had permitted relatively free elections in Jordan to place in power an Arab nationalist government headed by Suleiman Nabulsi, began having second thoughts. Without question the Nabulsi government saw its role as one of bringing about a more or less gradual merger of Jordan with the Arab nation, whose leader was Gamal Abdul Nasser. Hossein began to resist this policy and then suddenly executed a royal coup d'état and suppressed the Arab nationalist leaders. These actions and the desire to please Britain helped lead to a fundamental reassessment of the situation in the Arab Middle

East. Now the inferred answer to the question could be: "Not necessarily; with strong Anglo-American support traditional Arab leaders can carry out the kind of economic reform programs that will attract popular support and produce political stability."

As it had in the late summer of 1956, the American government once again had a policy toward the Arab Middle East that appeared to be consistent in its assumptions. But the two sets of assumptions were almost polar opposites. This time too the policy was short-lived. The first setback occurred in the fall of 1957 with the failure of an attempted coup against the pro-Nasser modernist-nationalist regime of Syria. Arabs generally believe this coup was American-sponsored and if the documents revealed at the trial of General Daghestani in Iraq in 1958 can be believed they are probably correct. In any event the reaction to this attempt was a suppression of Syrian moderates and a sharp move to the left within the Syrian government. In fact there is reason to believe that if Syria had not merged with Egypt shortly later to form the United Arab Republic, Syria would have passed under communist control.

Weeks later King Saud of Saudi Arabia was successfully accused of promoting an incredibly crude assassination plot against Nasser. Whether true or not, the accusation was used by Saud's enemies in his own court, and his eclipse soon followed. His brother, the present King Faisal, who at that time was unwilling to stand against Nasser, moved into a position of predominance.

Then in the spring of 1958 dissatisfaction with the bitterly anti-Nasser President Chamoun of Lebanon spilled over into open civil war. And finally in July of 1958 the Iraqi regime was suddenly toppled by a military coup d'état. Nuri as-Said was murdered, as was the king, and Iraq had a modernist-nationalist regime although, as events were to demonstrate, not a pro-Nasser one.

The grand climax of this policy was the sending of American marines into Lebanon and British troops into Jordan to support these tottering regimes. This was an obvious admission of failure and an equally obvious admission of assumptional error. But at least American policy was not troubled by the need to adhere to rigid doctrine. Although the Eisenhower Doctrine was not formally invoked in July, 1958, the Eisenhower administration made clear its conviction that Chamoun's request for military support was in accord with the terms of that doctrine. By the terms of the doctrine the United States agrees to come to the assistance of a Middle East state asking for assistance to resist an attack from the Soviet Union or a communist-dominated state. Presumably, therefore, the leaders of the Lebanese rebels were agents of communist aggression. Yet in one of the most spectacular reversals in American diplomatic history, and certainly one of the least noted, American diplomacy helped engineer the establishment in Lebanon of a coalition government in which one of the two most prominent rebel leaders was selected as premier. President Chamoun was compelled to give up his ambitions to succeed himself and Lebanon has been careful ever since to associate itself with the aims of Arab nationalism. The final irony is that a prime ingredient working for Nasser's leadership—the perceived external enemy—was weakened once the United States and Britain dropped their policy of open opposition to Nasser and the Arabs understood this policy change. Divisive forces within the modernist-nationalist movement manifested themselves and there followed an almost steady erosion of Nasser's support.

The picture that emerges is not one of an American policy that denied the relevance of Arab nationalism for the achievement of American containment objectives in the Middle East. But there is little to indicate that a fundamental situational analysis was made of Arab politics and of the direction of change on which a carefully conceived long-term strategy could be based. Instead, at each critical juncture the decision made seems to have been dictated by the exigencies of the moment and the personal reactions of the decision makers. This, rather than a careful reassessment of fundamental situational assumptions, could explain the contradiction of in effect defending Nasser in October, 1956, and then trying to isolate and destroy him in 1957. The Dulles-Eisenhower response to the Anglo-French-Israeli invasion of Egypt seems more likely to have been due to pique, distrust, and offended sensibilities directed against America's allies than to have been a part of a long-range strategy. And the opportunity offered by the disaffection of King Saud of Saudi Arabia and King Hossein of Jordan with Nasser in 1957 seems to have produced the decision to try to isolate Nasser through the Eisenhower Doctrine.

American diplomacy in the Suez crisis was of course in large part a reflection of the personality and diplomatic style of John Foster Dulles; and Dulles would have been exceptional in any age. It demonstrates that, despite the huge foreign policy bureaucracy today, a single individual can dominate important policy in a manner fully comparable to that of his eighteenth- and nineteenth-century predecessors. There is nothing to suggest, however, that Secretary Dulles was acting against the advice of a bureaucracy that had made an operational situational analysis and based on this had drawn up a long-term strategy reconciling fundamental objectives and capabilities. Indeed cases such as that of South Vietnam, where elements of the bureaucracy seem to have been central in decision-making, differ not at all in the ad hoc quality of their approach.

The South Vietnam crisis in the summer of 1963 illustrates this point. Unlike that in the Suez crisis, policy-making this time was not clearly in the hands of a single senior official. The periodic trips of General Maxwell Taylor and Secretary of Defense Robert McNamara to Saigon seemed to be an almost frantic search for a policy but one that amounted to more of an exhortation than a strategy. American officials were directed to take energetic measures to provide for a stable, anticommunist regime capable of defeating the Vietcong. But this was no more than a statement of well-understood aims; in no sense was it a strategy.

Inevitably different elements of the American foreign policy community concerned with South Vietnam came up with different tactical schemes for achieving the general policy objective.[9] These various schemes doubtlessly reflected the perceptual differences of individuals performing different roles. Confronted with clear evidence of an unpopular regime, which was only casual in its prosecution of the war against the Vietcong, American officials could have reasonably advanced three major alternative tactical schemes: to increase military, economic, and political support for the regime; to pressure Diem into making the kinds of social, economic, and political reform necessary to broaden his support; and to support a coup d'état. Thanks to some surprisingly good journalistic reporting, there is a good deal of evidence to support a contention that the first two tactical schemes had vigorous bureaucratic proponents and that United States policy ultimately backed into the third alternative more in acquiescence than in advocacy—certainly not with direction.[10]

Journalistic accounts make clear the point that the policy conflict was not merely interagency, centering on the Defense Department, the Department of State, and the Central Intelligence Agency, but *intra*agency as well. The picture that emerges of the C.I.A. role is particularly revealing. A crystallizing image of the C.I.A. in the American intellectual community is that of a right-wing organization with little concern for liberal values. This is at best a gross distor-

9. *The New York Times,* September 22, 1963, p. 3.

10. For some excellent accounts of intrabureaucratic bickering see the articles of Richard Starnes of Scripps Howard, David Halberstam and Max Frankel of the *New York Times,* and Malcolm W. Browne of the Associated Press in the summer of 1963.

tion, and in the Vietnam case the C.I.A. obviously could not be viewed as a monolith. Yet this image, distorted though it may be, is understandable.

What emerges from newspaper accounts concerning Vietnam in 1963 is that the number-one advocate of total support for Diem was John Richardson, the head of the C.I.A. in Saigon.[11] Apparently Richardson was deeply involved in and committed to intelligence liaison relations with, and paramilitary support of, the Diem government. This included giving financial support for the Vietnamese special services, the most loyal of the Diem security forces. Richardson's role therefore logically called for all-out support for Diem and no other policy recommendation should have been expected from him. This example leads to a conclusion regarding the C.I.A. which may help explain the right-wing image. Whenever American relations are close enough with a regime to establish liaison intelligence relations and paramilitary support, the C.I.A. as the involved agency will be predisposed to regard the perpetuation of that regime as essential to American security. Since such regimes are often right-wing, the C.I.A. finds itself frequently in visible relationships with right-wing regimes. But C.I.A. officers not involved in liaison work or paramilitary support will not necessarily be predisposed to support the regime. In the Vietnam case those officers who were in contact with opposition elements may even have been predisposed to favoring a coup d'état. Since the journalists writing from South Vietnam did not reveal their inside sources, there is no evidence to support a conjecture that a policy dispute raged within the C.I.A., but an analysis of the roles of those involved leads to the expectation that disputes along several lines occurred.

The case of General Paul Harkins, the senior American military

11. For articles on the close connection of Richardson and the Diem regime see *The New York Times,* October 4, 1963, p. 1, and October 6, 1963, Sec. 4, p. 8.

official in Saigon, is similar to that of Richardson. Intimately associated, as he had to be, with the Ngo brothers and their closest military advisors, Harkins' strong support of Diem [12] is easily explained. However, the liaison relationship for the American military need not always lead to an advocacy of support for a government. Since many Vietnamese officers were anti-Diem, their influence on American officers attached to their units led to disillusionment and hostility from some American military leaders. These men were unquestionably the sources for many of the journalistic reports of deep dissatisfaction in South Vietnam.[13]

Of the three primary American agencies represented in Saigon the one with the least role commitment to the Diem regime was the Department of State. But, as will be discussed in the final section of this study, the historical style of the Department of State is more that of the observer than of the activist. It is therefore not surprising that prior to the appointment of Henry Cabot Lodge as ambassador the Department of State was correct in its behavior. With the appointment of Lodge from outside the department, however, came the advocacy of a much tougher line with the Diem regime.[14] And when that government failed to heed American advice, a decision to press for significant personnel changes was made by the American government. President Kennedy underscored that line on September 2, 1963, in a *New York Times* interview.[15] Well understood was the point that the American government believed that Ngo Dinh Nhu, the brother of President Diem and leader of the C.I.A.-supported special services, should be removed. This conclusion was given further credence with the transfer of Richardson from South Vietnam. Whether the United States was directly in-

12. *Ibid.,* September 22, 1963, p. 3.
13. For examples in *The New York Times* see June 10, 1963, p. 1; July 3, 1963, p. 1; July 7, 1963, Sec. 4, p. 5; August 24, 1963, p. 2; August 26, 1963, p. 3.
14. *Ibid.,* September 12, 1963, p. 1.
15. *Ibid.,* September 3, 1963, p. 1.

volved in the coup d'état that followed is pragmatically and morally irrelevant. South Vietnamese officers had every right to believe a drastic governmental change would be welcomed in Washington.

The purpose of this brief glance at the American role in Vietnam at the time of Diem's overthrow is to explore the possibility that where the conduct of foreign policy is essentially in the hands of the bureaucracy, policy is less ad hoc and reflects greater long-range planning than when a single individual is firmly in control. If such were the case in Vietnam indications of it should have appeared with the replacement of Diem by the generally respected and well-liked General Duong Van (Big) Minh. Since the new regime was well disposed to receive American advice, it is justifiable at this point to look for evidence of what that advice was. What policy changes did Big Minh inaugurate to attract a broadly based coalition in support of his regime? What kind of an economic and social program was inaugurated? Answers to these questions should indicate the direction of change in Vietnam perceived by American bureaucratic analysts. In fact, however, policy changes appear to have been remarkably insignificant. True enough, Buddhist persecution ceased, political prisoners were released, and some personnel changes were made. But the new government's policy on the whole differed very little from that of its predecessor. To say that the popular base of support for the regime must be broadened is to say very little. Such a statement becomes meaningful only when answers are given to the questions of which specific groups are to be attracted and by what specific policies. In fact the South Vietnamese military junta that replaced President Diem seemed to be classifiable in that category of officers Samuel Finer describes as incapable of formulating a broad governmental program.[16]

The American role in South Vietnam falls into an increasingly clear pattern. Just as in Iran and Guatemala, where American

16. Samuel E. Finer, *The Man on Horseback* (New York, 1962), pp. 14–17.

involvement in the overturn of regimes is no longer questioned, there appears to have been in South Vietnam an almost total reliance on a few individuals as the answer to fundamental socio-political problems. Surely the perpetuation of this pattern is not due to spectacularly successful performances in Iran or Guatemala. Few could have wished to use General Zahedi of Iran or Castillo Armas of Guatemala as models for Big Minh's emulation in Saigon. Circumstantial evidence argues that American officials, with the great influence they had in the first post-Diem government, were without suggested solutions to the problems of attracting peasants, labor, and intellectual support to the South Vietnamese regime. The kind of careful, detailed situational analysis that would be a necessary preliminary to any such suggestions had probably not been made. As such the only difference between the handling of the Suez crisis and the one in South Vietnam lies with the locus of decision-making. In the Suez case, a strong Secretary of State obviously dominated the decision-making process. In South Vietnam policy emerged from an intrabureaucratic conflict in which President Kennedy seems to have been the arbiter. But the essential style was the same.

If the intuitive and ad hoc style of diplomacy has remained constant over the years, there has been a substantial stylistic change in the realm of interference in the domestic affairs of other states. The few cases of American interference in which governments fell as a consequence are only the most spectacular manifestations of a pervasive mode of diplomatic behavior. But this common propensity to interfere is only symptomatic of what John Herz refers to as the passing of the era of territorial impermeability.[17] In the years before the nation-state era interference was equally common. In those years, however, interference was interoligarchical and was largely confined to the various courts. Quite sensibly, individuals and fac-

17. John Herz, *International Politics in the Atomic Age* (New York, 1959).

tions were the primary concern. Interference in an age of mass politics is infinitely more complex and demands a comprehensive understanding of social, economic, and political forces and trends. But given the prevailing diplomatic style, current interference with its predisposition to focus on individuals is carried out in a manner befitting the early eighteenth century.

The contention that the current style of diplomacy is no longer adequate implies a need for a theoretical base for diplomacy. But the insight and understanding of the experienced diplomat are indispensable ingredients as much for the diplomacy of the future as for the diplomacy of the past. To conclude that the individual diplomat, regardless of competence, is not capable of knowing all that must be known in any particular situation and that he requires a firm theoretical foundation from which to work should in no way denigrate his role. A diplomacy based on a rigid recipe application of a theoretical model would be far worse than one based on the intuitive skill of the experienced diplomat.

ULTIMATE RECOURSE

War is commonly thought of as the ultimate recourse for states involved in irreconcilable conflict. There is nothing implicit in such a conception that demands that guns must be fired and people must die. The term "Cold War" is in no way a misnomer. It means that the ultimate recourse available to the primary combatants, given their understanding of the horrors of nuclear war, is a course of action in which limited shooting engagements play a subsidiary role. Despite the general acceptance of the term "Cold War," however, there is a tendency to think of the Cold War as not a "real" war. Real war for most people is total war.

A characteristic feature of the mass-politics era is the absolute flavor of the concept of war. In earlier times the mass of the population, though often victims of warfare, were disinterested observers when not in the line of march. As political awareness spread in Europe and America, the values of national independence, dignity, and prestige were widely accepted and entire populations identified with their governments. With this mass involvement has come the expression of conflicting national aims and aspirations in terms of right and wrong, good and evil. And flowing naturally from this has been the popular demand for total victory. In fact, the point has been reached at which total war implies literally a life and death struggle for peoples organized in states.

Since World War II political awareness has increased at an accelerating rate and has spread into previously unconcerned populations in Asia, Africa, and Latin America. A logical assumption therefore is that World War III would differ from World War II primarily in the greater population involvement in the former. The logic of this assumption collapses, however, when the incredible destructive power of thermonuclear weapons is considered. Quite obviously neither western nor Soviet leaders regard the inaugurating of total warfare as an option. It now seems reasonable to hope that the era of total war began and ended in the first half of the twentieth century.

At the same time, the conflict of aims and aspirations of the communist and noncommunist blocs has been as nearly irreconcilable as any major dispute in history. Even with the liberalization trend in the Soviet Union, the Sino-Soviet split, and the beginnings of agreements designed to reduce the likelihood of accidental all-out war, few in the West doubt that, given the opportunity, either the Soviet Union or Communist China would expand its domain.

What then is the ultimate recourse to which these antagonists can turn? Some see the answer in limited warfare. Many studies have been written, some of them excellent, concerning the strategy of limited warfare. But most of them point out that limited warfare, whether conventional or nuclear, would be difficult to control. The process of escalation could too easily result in the very thermonuclear contest the antagonists wish to avoid. Consequently it can be assumed that none will lightly undertake limited warfare engagements and therefore that such engagements will only occasionally constitute the ultimate recourse.

As this conclusion has been increasingly accepted, the focus of attention has shifted one level down to guerrilla warfare and to outside support of, or opposition to, insurrectionists. This type of activity can be reasonably described as ultimate recourse since a losing side may well prefer defeat to the risk of escalating the conflict. But here again this level of conflict cannot account for more than a small percentage of final engagements in the Cold War, for guerrilla warfare and insurrection are likely to occur only sporadically.

A major contention of this study is that the great bulk of final Cold War engagements have occurred and will continue to occur below the level of shooting warfare. Ultimate recourse today, whether recognized as such or not, is to be found primarily on the levels of political warfare, economic warfare, and psychological warfare. The field of battle now extends widely into what, in a simpler age, were thought to be areas of exclusive sovereign concern. With the diffusion of the concept of ultimate recourse, highly critical Cold War battles are occurring as part of the domestic political process of every state, whether it be great or of only slight significance.

This conclusion suggests why a style of diplomacy that was well adapted to the needs of eighteenth-century interstate relations and was increasingly inadequate but still tolerable in the nineteenth and early twentieth centuries is now both inadequate and intolerable. The essential purpose of diplomacy for any government is to gain some influence over those policies of the target government that are considered to be relevant to the national security and welfare. In the eighteenth and much of the nineteenth centuries, the decision-making process for those policies of primary concern to a foreign government was likely to involve a limited number of men within an aristocracy, and diplomats would be in contact with these men. Therefore a state of diplomacy that relied upon the skill and sensitivity of individual diplomats was appropriate. With the growth of political awareness, however, the decision-making process became increasingly complex and individual policy makers found their freedom of action steadily reduced. Logically, a government seeking to influence the policy of another government should, at this point, have expanded its scope of activities to attempt to influence decision-making at levels other than the top governmental. It is understandable that this was done very little, however. The style of diplomacy was well established and, since the change in the political process occurred gradually, there was no point at which the inadequacy of the earlier diplomatic style came into sharp focus. In fact, the most influential of post-World War II analysts of diplomatic style, Hans Morgenthau, argues implicitly that the inadequacy of style in the 1950's could best be remedied by a closer approximation of the eighteenth-century model.[18] Furthermore, any changes in style in the direction of influencing policy at critical points other than the top governmental would have involved expanded interference, and one of the characteristic features of a mass-politics society is a nationalism with little tolerance for such interference.

The difference between tolerable and intolerable inadequacy, then, lies with the difference in levels of ultimate recourse. In the 1930's the diplomatic failure to influence aggressive German policy led to a referral of the contest to the ultimate recourse of total war. In the 1960's such a referral is impossible if civilization is to survive and in most instances the arena of diplomacy is the locale for ultimate recourse. Failure there is final failure.

Henry Kissinger in his *Nuclear Weapons and Foreign Policy*

18. See Hans Morgenthau, *Politics Among Nations,* 3d ed. (New York, 1960), Pt. 10.

develops the point that status quo governments are at a diplomatic disadvantage in dealing with revolutionary governments.[19] In fact, this point is made so strongly that the reader would be justified in concluding that, in a purely diplomatic contest between two governments of comparable power, victory for the revolutionary over the status quo is almost inevitable. If the contention is accurate that ultimate recourse today will be largely at a diplomatic level, this conclusion should be a disconcerting one for the western reader. Happily though, there is much reason to doubt the sweeping nature of Kissinger's analysis. The dichotomy he draws between the status quo government, assuming good faith and striving for compromise as an end, and the revolutionary government, monolithic, highly rational, and viewing a compromise as merely a tactical delay in the long strategic road, is much too absolute. One of the conclusions of this study, nevertheless, is that in the early years of the Cold War era communist diplomacy does have an advantage. This advantage is not a genetic one, characteristic of revolutionary governments generally, nor is it unalterable; but it is significant enough to call for a drastic revision of the western diplomatic style.

The communist advantage can be seen by looking at three problems that stand in the path of an alteration of western diplomatic style. First, the new form of ultimate recourse demands a level of sophistication and situational understanding far exceeding that of any previous era. Total warfare, with unconditional surrender by the enemy as its objective, had an implicit simplicity. What is called for now is a detailed understanding of the socio-political-economic situation, including the major trends of that situation for every state in the world. Without such an understanding, a strategy designed to influence trends in a direction favorable to western objectives could not be devised. The failure of western governments to make the kind of situational analyses that are opera-

19. Henry Kissinger, *Nuclear Weapons and Foreign Policy* (New York, 1958).

tionally useful is not a reflection of incompetence in the areas concerned. The United States government, for example, now has voluminous and detailed, if bland and unfocused, country studies of every area of the world. The reason for the lack of operational focus in these studies is a circular one. Given the current diplomatic style, there is little awareness of a need for operational focus and thus little demand for making these studies so.

Second, clandestine political warfare of the type called for raises ethical questions of fundamental importance. Because of the prevailing values in the West, the very notion of this kind of involvement in the domestic politics of other peoples is ethically offensive. A basic element in the failure to develop a theoretical base for interference is doubtlessly due to an unwillingness to accept the need for interference as continuing policy.

Third, the conduct of political warfare requires a foreign policy bureaucracy that has the freedom of action to carry out intricately involved tactical maneuvers. The Vietnamese case outlined above would seem to show that the American foreign policy bureaucracy is granted the necessary freedom of action by default. Since only a tiny element of the American population has the understanding of a situation such as that in Vietnam to come to an informed opinion about American foreign policy, the bureaucracy would appear to have a free hand. But this conclusion does not take account of the boundary-constructing role that the public plays in the foreign policy process. Although even the politically interested elements of western democracies cannot understand the complexities and subtleties of current world disputes, the intensity of public concern in the outcome of the conflict with the Soviet Union and China is as great as that of previous generations who were involved in seemingly irreconcilable conflicts. Consequently the simplistic black and white images of opponents, which are characteristic of the mass-politics era generally, have been constructed. But this time an easily understood victory over the absolute foe is most unlikely.

Instead the objectives of battles that will be fought will be largely incomprehensible to all but the best informed and most sophisticated. Popular bewilderment and dissatisfaction are therefore inevitable, and any democratic administration will be under strong pressure, particularly in election years, to relieve the resulting frustrations by taking clear-cut and decisive action.

What this amounts to in practical terms is that the foreign policy bureaucracy must avoid adopting a strategic and tactical scheme that can be interpreted as appeasement or as damaging to national prestige. This restriction applies even with regard to policy in areas that are out of the public eye. A serious diplomatic defeat in an obscure area will quickly destroy its obscurity and will lead to a searching appraisal by opposition party leaders to see if there is evidence of appeasement or something worse. The Congo crisis, which became a matter of American domestic political dispute, illustrates this point. Since any policy other than one of unequivocal hostility to communist or neutralist regimes and unequivocal support for vociferously anticommunist regimes is open to an interpretation as appeasement by the American public, the boundaries to freedom of action for the American foreign policy bureaucracy can be very restrictive. These boundaries are immediately restrictive, however, only in those areas of greatest public interest, for example, American policy toward Castro and Communist China. In other areas the boundaries are only potentially restrictive and here policy makers may be willing to pursue a tactical scheme that involves some risk of being interpreted as appeasement.

These three obstacles to developing a more effective diplomatic style are not to be found in comparable degree in the Soviet Union and Communist China. First of all, whereas the ad hoc and intuitive approach of western diplomacy has concealed the need for an operationally useful situational analysis, the communist diplomats are predisposed to value such analyses. The scientific mystique of the Marxist diplomat calls for the construction of a socio-political-economic picture of a target society and of its expected dialectical development. Policy is then reconciled to this picture. Doctrinal presuppositions may well result in serious distortions of the actual situation in some cases,[20] and it should be considered that in all cases the interpretation of the situation will be one that suits Soviet or Chinese purposes. But an analysis will at least be made, and sometimes that analysis will be remarkably perceptive, particularly with regard to developing countries.[21]

The ethical problem implicit in interference is not nearly as important for communist states as it is for the United States. Since national values are of no permanent importance in Marxist theory and the state itself is seen as a temporary phenomenon, the communist doctrinaire considers the ethics of interference per se to be irrelevant. This conclusion can be carried too far. Conflicts within the communist world demonstrate clearly enough that interference is still resented by communist governments. But there is likely to be far less reluctance in the Soviet Union and China to develop strategic and tactical schemes involving interference in the affairs of other states than there is in the United States.

On the third point there is no basis for comparison. The mass of the Soviet and Chinese people quite obviously have few means at hand to influence their governments to pursue any particular policy. Consequently the boundaries placed around the behavior of the communist foreign policy bureaucracy are almost as broad as those in a pre-mass politics society.

The popular restrictions on freedom of action of the foreign policy bureaucracy in a western democracy may lead to frustrations and an inability to pursue what bureaucratic experts regard as the best strategy for achieving objectives. These restrictions,

20. Marshall D. Shulman, *Stalin's Foreign Policy Reappraised* (Cambridge, Mass., 1963), pp. 264–71.

21. For an example of an acute analysis of Iran's political development and Soviet and Iranian communist tactical errors see the Tudeh Party publication "Twenty Eight Mordad," a booklet distributed clandestinely in 1954.

however, are part of the liberal democratic process and no advocate of liberal democracy would call for a policy of insulating the foreign policy bureaucrat from popular pressure. Nor does Soviet experience show that a bureaucracy which need not worry about the public's attitude is likely to produce a more effective policy.[22] Doctrinal distortion and bureaucratic parochialism are characteristic problems for foreign policy formulation when the public is not involved.

RELUCTANCE TO INTERFERE

Thus far in the discussion of popular restrictions on foreign policy, the public referred to has been that large section of the population which participates in politics to the extent of voting and is only vaguely concerned with and informed about foreign policy. The voice of this group is only sporadically heard on foreign affairs and then usually because of some seriously damaging action to national prestige or because of personal involvement, as through conscription or mobilization. Its influence on most policies is simply the consequence of policy makers' realization that the group holds political potential. But the section of the population that Gabriel Almond calls the "attentive public"[23] has a far more active role to play. This 10 or 15 per cent of the population is concerned enough to be informed about the general flow of foreign policy and some of the more important specific problems. As such this group has the important functions of watching and criticizing the conduct of foreign affairs. These responsibilities, however, are not being carried out as well as they should be in this era, for two major reasons. First, because of the great complexity of every aspect of foreign policy today, the attentive public increasingly lacks the competence to make informed criticisms. Second, the attentive public generally

22. See Shulman, *Stalin's Foreign Policy Reappraised,* for evidence of this.
23. Gabriel Almond, *The American People and Foreign Policy* (New York, 1950).

finds interfering in the affairs of others ethically repulsive. When confronted with a necessity to interfere, the governmental elite, which for the most part shares this public attitude, does so but only when no alternative can be found. The attentive public prefers to ignore such lapses if at all possible. Yet, given the extraordinary danger of escalation, the conclusion is inescapable that ultimate recourse in the Cold War period must often take the form of competitive interference. If the boundaries set by the American public in the foreign policy field are such as to limit the American government to crisis interference, American capability will have been seriously and adversely affected.

The reluctance to interfere in the affairs of other peoples is easily understandable. National self-determination remains an integral part of the liberal faith, and interference clearly contradicts this principle. The advocacy of national self-determination was an outgrowth of the utilitarian assumption of a natural harmony of interest: if a people can become a nation that is truly independent and free of domestic tyranny, the nation then will be able to live in peace and harmony in a world community of like nations. For the liberal, respect for the dignity of the national personality was as valid an end as respect for the dignity of the individual personality. Nationalism, which calls for the independence, dignity, and prestige of the nation, was therefore intimately connected with liberalism, which asked the same for the individual.

This doctrine received supreme expression in Wilson's Fourteen Points and shocking refutation in the phenomenon of fascism. Hitler demonstrated conclusively enough that when the collective values of nationalism conflict with the individual values of liberalism, the result may be the subversion of the latter. The conclusion that could be, and to some extent was, drawn from Nazism therefore was that national values and individual values need not be part of the same ideological parcel and in fact could easily conflict. After World War II certainly very few believed a natural harmony of interest to be a base for national self-determination. The postwar school of thought that dominated the academic and practitioner alike in the area of foreign affairs was the realist school, which asserted the primacy of national power interests in determining international behavior. Discarded along with the idea of a natural harmony of interest of free and independent nations was the focus on the ultimate value of the dignity of the individual personality—a somewhat strange development considering the anti-individualist value system of the fascist enemy.

However, the basis of the attraction of the realist school was probably less in the compelling nature of its logic—the determinism implicit in its supposition that national leaders will pursue the power interests of their nation was never developed—than in a reaction to the weak diplomacy that did so little to contain fascism. In any event the assumption of the oneness of liberalism and national self-determination persisted, although rarely explicitly, as an atavistic but attitude-determining force. The *Nation* magazine, for example, which has few kind words for American nationalism, reacted to the Bay of Pigs failure with the assertion that all inter-ference is bad and to be avoided.[24] If the ultimate goal is for a government to be liberal and supranational, however, the *Nation's* stricture against any interference (including presumably that car-ried out against an illiberal regime) is no less of a reactionary throwback than an argument against the right of the federal govern-ment to interfere with the southern states in order to compel them to accept desegregation.

The conclusion, of course, is not that interference is desirable. Whether any act of interference is good or bad is a value judgment that could be based logically on the type of interference and the ends for which the interference is conducted. An absolute char-acterization of interference as bad makes sense only for those who consider the inviolability of the nation a supreme value. Even in the

24. See *The Nation,* Vol. 192 (May 6, 1961), p. 383.

era in which national self-determination was an article of faith, interference was commonly resorted to.[25] Today, with communist competitors paying little attention to national boundaries, to be unwilling to interfere even in defense of liberal democratic regimes is to be remarkably doctrinaire. In actual behavior few if any Americans are that doctrinaire regarding interference. This conclusion can be illustrated by comparing the reactions in the United States to the Cuban misadventure of April, 1961, and the support given by the United States to United Nations interference in Katanga. Those who opposed interference in principle with regard to Cuba generally supported the Katanga interference, whereas those who criticized the Cuban operation only in that it was not extensive enough deplored in principle the interference in Katanga.[26] Supporters of the Katanga interference might argue that there is a fundamental difference between American unilateral intervention and the United Nation's collective intervention. But these people raised no objections to, and in fact generally applauded, the unconcealed American interference in the Dominican Republic directed against a restoration of the Trujillo family.[27] This does not mean that arguments against interference are simply a matter of convenience. On the contrary, those arguments are forgotten only when a goal is clearly prior to and in conflict with the principle of the inviolability of a nation.

The need for a clear-cut ethic regarding interference per se is a compelling one. Confusion over the ethics of interference leads to

25. See D. A. Graber, *Crisis Diplomacy* (Washington, 1959).

26. See *The New Republic,* Vol. 145 (October 2, 1961), pp. 3–5; *The Nation,* Vol. 195 (November 24, 1962), p. 339; E. V. Kuchnelt-Leddihn, "What about Katanga," *The National Review,* Vol. 11 (October 21, 1961), p. 266.

27. See, for example, Rayford W. Logen, "Dominican Republic: Struggle for Tomorrow," *The Nation,* Vol. 193 (December 16, 1961), pp. 488–90; Thomas P. Whitney, "The U.S. and the Dominicans," *The New Republic,* Vol. 146 (February 12, 1962), p. 13; Rowland Evans, Jr., "First Steps in Dominican Democracy," *The Reporter,* Vol. 28 (January 3, 1963), p. 21.

serious difficulties in determining goals and in long-term strategic planning. Typically, the American foreign policy maker will turn to crude interference when the exigencies of a crisis compel him to; but once the immediate crisis has passed he will seek to withdraw from all but the gentlest form of interference. He will assume that by his simple act of interference the problem has been solved and that a long-term strategic plan that includes tactical interference is not necessary.

These points can be illustrated by the case of the overthrow of the Arbenz government of Guatemala in 1954. There is now general acceptance of the conclusion that the United States government gave active support to the rebel movement of Castillo Armas. This action was in response to the firm conviction that under Arbenz Guatemala was rapidly becoming a communist state and, as such, a clear threat to American security. Undoubtedly there were alternatives to this type of drastic interference. No regime is ever monolithic, and in Guatemala in 1954 there were many anticommunist or at least non-communist individuals or groups who might have been able to alter the trend toward communism if American backing, overt and covert, had been forthcoming. Even assuming, however, that alternatives were in fact considered before the United States reluctantly concluded that the trend was so strong in the direction of communism that only outside intervention could reverse it, the placing of total reliance on Castillo Armas, given American objectives, was an act of irresponsibility.

When a government of a minor state owes its very existence to support from another, greater power, that government's patriotism is certain to be questioned by some sections of the populace as long as nationalism is important. A widespread conclusion that the regime is guilty of treason can be avoided only if that regime pursues foreign and domestic policies which are likely to have a broad appeal. An interfering great power would therefore be unwise if it did not use its influence to establish and strengthen trends toward a more broadly acceptable regime. In 1954 the Guatemalan citizen was thoroughly justified in watching the behavior of the Castillo Armas government for indications that American interference was truly disinterested and that the welfare and freedom of the Guatemalan people were primary concerns. Gaining broad acceptance for Castillo Armas, particularly in Guatemala City, would have been difficult at best because Arbenz was associated with the Arevalo revolutionary movement, which had a good deal of popularity. There is little visible evidence, however, to indicate that the American government in fact had sought to assert real control over the Castillo Armas government. All-out support does not provide control. In a similar situation in Iran, the American-supported premier, Fazlollah Zahedi, could hardly have followed a less appealing policy line. In both cases American policy in effect selected a man as an answer to a crisis situation and then gave him full backing. The results in Guatemala were better than Americans had any right to expect. The results in Iran were no worse.

A reasonable reconstruction of the decision to interfere in Guatemala could be the following: By early 1954 the urgency of the Guatemalan situation could no longer be denied. Communist influence in government, labor, and the countryside was steadily increasing and the likelihood that Guatemala would soon be a major center of communist subversion in Latin America was a very real one.[28] The threat to American security interests was judged to be extremely serious, obviously calling for an energetic course of action. Castillo Armas, already engaged in intensive anti-Arbenz maneuvers among Guatemalan exile groups, presented a ready-made answer. He and his group were anticommunist and their vested interests would keep them so. The fact that there were in this group many men whose social and economic philosophies, if translated into public policy, would likely increase the country's

28. Robert J. Alexander, *Communism in Latin America* (New Brunswick, N. J., 1957), pp. 361–64.

receptivity for communism was probably not seen as a matter of consequence. Failure in such a venture, of course, could lead to a rapid consolidation of communist power, but the American government clearly regarded the situation as serious enough to warrant such a risk. Backing for Castillo Armas was total and unequivocal and, as will be argued below, such a policy was certain to weaken the American bargaining position.

Official documents concerning this policy will not be available for a great many years; therefore it is possible only to conjecture what alternatives to this policy were considered. A good guess is that they fell into two categories: those aimed at overthrowing the Arbenz government and those aimed at working through normal diplomatic channels to oppose and isolate Arbenz. The area of alternatives probably not considered was that of less drastic forms of interference, designed to alter the trends toward communist domination, yet this is the type of action that could best combine effectiveness with low risk. It is true that a strategy involving continuing interference calls for an extremely good understanding of the situation and a highly skilled staff, but the lack of either or both of these is not the primary obstacle to adopting policy along this line. The primary obstacle is the unwillingness, for ethical reasons or because of a well-established style of diplomacy, to adopt a policy that involves continuing interference. Only in the area of economic aid is a policy of planned interference designed to alter trends of development commonly accepted; here acceptance is possible because it is not generally admitted that economic aid constitutes interference.

By avoiding a strategy that involves continuing interference, the policy maker does not avoid the necessity to interfere. On the contrary, since little is done to alter dangerous trends while they are developing, avoidable crises occur and, unhappily, a policy of gross interference is commonly employed to deal with the situation. When the crisis has passed there is a return to the stance of noninterference. This policy of crisis interference followed by a period of virtual noninterference is most unlikely to achieve intended results. Overturning a regime is the easy part of political engineering. Creating a stable, popular, and ideologically compatible regime is infinitely more complex and seems at this stage to be beyond the theoretical competence of the United States. Yet the probability remains that the United States will be increasingly involved in operations that can be described as competitive interference and that a failure to perform well in these operations could be decisive in the Cold War.

If the Department of State building is seen as symbolic of the successful aspects of the American response to the modern diplomatic challenge, the Central Intelligence Agency building in McLean, Virginia, can be viewed as symbolic of the failures. Standing in grand isolation eight miles from Foggy Bottom, the C.I.A. building signifies a failure to integrate covert and overt diplomacy. For official as well as unofficial Americans, the necessity to resort to covert diplomacy is accepted only sporadically and then nervously and with embarrassment. Placing the agency charged with responsibility for covert diplomacy away from the mainstream of Washington life is only apropos. Modern technology can easily overcome the communication problem imposed by physical separation. But the psychological separation is more difficult to bridge. The problem of replacing an ad hoc style of diplomacy with one that is based on a systematically developed and long-term-focused strategy is difficult enough; to have it compounded by institutional obstacles is doubly discouraging.

1 | TOLERANCE LEVELS OF INTERFERENCE

THE LATE nineteenth and early twentieth centuries witnessed a serious effort to regularize international behavior and to codify international legal practices. Implicit in this endeavor was an acceptance of the nation state as the primary organizational unit of world society. The implicit objective was the institutionalization of the status quo in this society of nation states. Since intervention by the government of one state in the affairs of another was highly disruptive of this status quo, defining and limiting intervention was a primary task for those seeking to regularize behavior. In approaching this problem they gave a good deal of thought to determining what constituted intervention and where the boundaries between legal and illegal intervention lay.[1] But the fairly substantial literature that appeared on this subject has little relevance to the problems of today.

A basic assumption of this study is that the era is now passing in which a society of self-contained nation states can be the primary

1. For a discussion of this topic and the views of various writers see Ann V. Thomas and A. J. Thomas, Jr., *Non-Intervention: The Law and its Impact in the Americas* (Dallas, Tex., 1956).

focus of the rules of behavior for a world society. That is not to say that nationalism will quickly subside everywhere. On the contrary, nationalism will surely remain throughout the next generation as a prime determinant of behavior in world society. But for a number of reasons state boundaries are unlikely to regain their pre-World War II significance. The technological revolution has resulted in communications improvements that are destroying world parochialism. The growth in economic interdependence is producing a world economy that must be viewed in its entirety. And many of the new states in Asia and Africa are so linguistically and ethnically diverse that they are not likely to develop within the European nation-state pattern. Finally, weapons systems have been developed that make interstate warfare on a shooting level increasingly risky and this leads to the increasing willingness to turn to intervention in an effort to win limited victories.

The extensive interfering in the domestic affairs of other states by the governments of most states is an important manifestation of the changed mode of world behavior. Despite this quantitative increase in interference, however, western diplomacy cannot be said to have adjusted to these fundamental changes. The West has great difficulty in not viewing interference both ethically and pragmatically in the context of the unchallenged nation-state era. As discussed in the introduction, an altering of this view is essential if the sporadic, crisis-associated, and hastily planned style of performance by the West in its acts of interference is to be avoided. But, of even greater importance, a meaningful accommodation with the communist powers can be reached only if this view is changed. Since highly critical Cold War battles are being fought in the form of competitive interference, any serious effort to reach a broad accommodation must focus on spelling out permissible and forbidden practices in this area. An effort must be made to determine which acts of interference should be outlawed in interstate practice. Hopefully as tensions ease the category of prohibited acts of interference can be expanded.[2] But it is unlikely that behavior in this area will ever again resemble that of the preatomic era.

In re-evaluating the role of interference a basic first step is to erase the distinction between what is loosely called "normal diplomatic behavior" and interference. To search for a fine line dividing normal diplomatic behavior, interference, and intervention is not only futile but tends to obscure the important point that there is a continuum from slight to intense interference. As used in this study "interference" is defined as any act by the government or the citizens of one state designed to influence the policy of the government of another state or to influence the internal developments of that state, whether they be political, economic, or social. Thus defined, interference would include both acts of persuasion and acts of coercion. Similarly, acts that are tolerated by a target government and people as well as those which are not would be classed as interference.

Some degree of interference by the government and/or citizens of one state in the affairs of another state is expected and will be tolerated by the target government and people. But when the type and degree of interference exceed expectations, the interfering state can expect a hostile reaction, which may have the immediate result of altering relations significantly. Each government and people will at any moment have a certain range of tolerance of interference. This range of tolerance can be defined at any particular time only by estimating the response to a number of acts of interference carried out for a variety of ends and by governments that have a wide variety of relationships with the target government. Such an estimate would indicate the categories of interference and maximum degree of interference within each category that a government and people will tolerate.

2. On this point see William T. Burke, "The Legal Regulation of Minor International Coercion: A Framework of Inquiry," in *Essays on Intervention,* ed. Roland J. Stranger (Columbus, Ohio, 1964).

The concept of a range of tolerance of interference has something of the same analytical and prescriptive utility in this era as did the concepts of normal diplomatic behavior and intervention in the previous era. In seeking to achieve their foreign policy objectives most western governments will prefer to utilize means that are well within the umbrella of what is regarded here as tolerated interference. This is close to saying that these governments prefer to follow normal diplomatic behavior. On occasion, however, they will feel compelled to resort to means that go beyond the target government's tolerance threshold and therefore by definition will stimulate a hostile reaction. This action is close to what was called illegal intervention before World War II. There is an analytically significant difference, however, in that the terms normal diplomatic behavior and intervention referred to sets of procedures that were felt to be distinctively separate, although there was overlapping. For example, the sending of troops into the territory of another state would be classified as intervention and the presenting of a démarche to a chief of state would be classified as normal diplomatic behavior. As defined here, interference covers both procedures and it is easily conceivable that in one situation the sending of armed forces would be welcomed by the target state, whereas the démarche in another situation could produce a hostile reaction. Furthermore, interference of a certain type and degree will be accepted in one relationship and not in another. From both an analytical and prescriptive point of view it is much more important to classify a diplomatic act on the basis of tolerance than of procedure. Crossing the threshold of tolerance of interference is a matter of deep concern pragmatically and ethically, but engaging in interference that is tolerated need not be.

Any nation's range of tolerance of interference is in constant flux, sometimes changing radically in a brief period. For example, the government and people of Egypt prior to the 1952 coup d'état could be classified as having an extraordinarily broad tolerance range, but after Nasser established his dictatorship that range narrowed sharply. On the other hand, liberal-minded Cubans who had violently opposed "Yankee imperialism" for generations found themselves suddenly in a position of pleading for American intervention against the Castro regime.[3] For most peoples, of course, the tolerance range is far more constant but for all it is in motion.

In the pages that follow the concept of range of tolerance of interference will be developed first by looking at ten types of interference that are commonly resorted to. The range of tolerance refers both to the types of interference that are tolerated and the degree of interference tolerated within each type. Second, a group of tentative hypotheses will be advanced suggesting variations in type and degree of interference that are likely to be tolerated in different relationship patterns. Third, a number of indicators will be suggested that can serve as a basis for predicting the general breadth of the range of tolerance of interference of any government and people at a particular time.

TYPES OF INTERFERENCE

The type of interference most commonly tolerated to some degree is that which is carried out through regular diplomatic channels and follows generally accepted diplomatic procedures. Even here the degree of tolerance frequently is insufficient for two governments to maintain diplomatic representatives in each other's capital city. But in such cases, unless the two governments have virtually no interest in each other, some form of diplomatic channel will be utilized to influence the other's policy. Sometimes this is done directly, as in the Warsaw meetings of American and Communist Chinese representatives. More commonly the channel will be through a third party with which both governments have diplo-

---

3. For an excellent study of the use made of anti-Yankee attitudes to destroy the liberal middle-class leadership see Tad Szulc and Karl E. Meyer, *The Cuban Invasion: The Chronicle of a Disaster* (New York, 1962).

matic relations. Any independent government, however, will have a tolerance limit for both the style and substance of diplomatic representations. A démarche can be so harshly or crudely phrased or a diplomat can attempt to influence policy or personnel selection on such a level as to generate a hostile response that could result in altering relations.

This type of interference is not always focused on immediate ends. Internal developmental trends of long- and short-term nature may be the objective instead. For example, the credits granted Poland are obviously designed to influence both the internal liberalization trend of Poland and the willingness of Poland to adopt a foreign policy stance with some independence of Moscow. These motives are certainly understood by the Polish government, yet this attempt to interfere is nonetheless tolerated.

For Americans in particular this is the favored type of interference. Procedurally it is inoffensive and, historically, actions of this variety were not thought of as intervention. Yet since this category includes economic, technical, and military aid it incorporates programs that have determined the direction of the political evolution of some states and has influenced substantially the development of most. Unpopular regimes have been maintained in power through such aid as was granted to Guatemala, Jordan, and Iran. Other more broadly based regimes, as in Turkey, Thailand, and Pakistan, owe much of their longevity to this type of support. And several democratic states, including some in western Europe, might well have suffered a change of regime without economic aid.

A second type of interference is less likely to meet with general acceptance and yet in most relationships is regarded as inoffensive. This is open educational and propagandizing activity by representatives or declared agents of one government with the citizenry of another, which is designed to create sentiment for certain policy lines. The degree of tolerance here depends on the type of material that is presented, the target group, and the policy ends. A good indicator of the degree of tolerance here is the ease with which information officer representatives of a government can communicate with, meet with, and entertain citizens of the host government, in particular the press corps. Broadcasts from official radio stations are included in this class of interference, as are most of the activities of such organizations as the United States Information Agency.

A third type falls under the heading of public statements made outside diplomatic channels either by officials or nonofficials of one state that appear to be designed to influence the policies of the government of another state. A great variety of statements, written or spoken, falls into this category and ranges from the innocuous and innocent to the officially threatening. In the 1930's Reza Shah of Iran threatened to break diplomatic relations with France because of an article critical of the Iranian regime that appeared in a French newspaper.[4] But this case represents the extreme narrowness of tolerance in this category. Many regimes maintain such a tight censorship that their citizens are unaware of critical statements made about their government abroad. In such cases nonofficial remarks are likely to be ignored. The extent of tolerance will vary, among other things, with the position held by the person making the statement, the intended target group and objective, the tone of the statement, the subject matter, and the communications channels utilized. A target government in its assessment of a statement will most certainly take into consideration the type of political process extant in the state in which the statement is made. The remarks of a private citizen of a totalitarian state may be assumed to be officially endorsed, but the remarks of a high-level bureaucrat of a democratic state may be regarded as a personal view. The accuracy of this assessment, however, will depend on the perceptual frame of those making the assessment and is often very faulty.

Closely resembling this type of interference but important enough

4. "Iran's Rupture with France," *Great Britain and the East,* Vol. 52 (1939), p. 94.

to warrant a separate category are public statements made outside diplomatic channels by officials or nonofficials of one state that indicate approval or disapproval of official personnel or aspirants to official positions of a government of another state. Again the variety of statements in this category is great and a lightly publicized remark of a private citizen is tolerated by almost any government. But, in general, the degree of tolerance for statements in this category is, in every relationship pattern, markedly less than in the previous category. When President Kennedy in 1963 alluded to the necessity for personnel changes in South Vietnam the world understood that he was risking a very sharp alteration of policy toward the United States by the Diem government despite the latter's dependence on American aid.

Many statements by officials or nonofficials that do have an impact on another government and/or people will not necessarily have been designed to influence the behavior of that government or people. Should the government or people so influenced believe that the statement was designed to effect their behavior, their reaction will nevertheless be identical to what it would be if the statement had in fact been designed to influence their behavior. The perception of intent is determining. Therefore such statements can be classified as inadvertent interference.

On the other hand if a government and people understand that a statement to which they have reacted was made purely for local consumption, it is not considered a case of interference. Rather, such statements influence the image a people will have of the state in which the statement originated. The image in turn is an important factor in determining the nature of a bilateral relationship. Statements of this variety can therefore have an indirect policy impact but not one resulting from an offended sense of propriety.

Another common type of interference is lobbying activities conducted by the government or citizens of one state, using citizens of the target state to alter policies of the government of that state.

There is a good deal of tolerance for such activity, as evidenced by the requirement that Americans engaged in such activity on behalf of a foreign government register as agents of that government. Americans, even some with political ambitions, do not feel that such activity is at all likely to hurt their public image.[5] But they obviously would not perform similar services for several categories of foreign governments. Excellent examples of the surprising degree of American tolerance for this practice were furnished by the Fulbright inquiry into such activities by foreign governments. The hearings of the Fulbright committee pointed to some very crude forms of lobbying on behalf of minor governments that are close allies of the United States.[6]

Overt efforts to remove bureaucratic personnel or to help elect a favored candidate is a type of interference that is tolerated far less. Possibly the most blatant activity of this sort in the United States was that carried out by the so-called China lobby, yet such activity did not alter United States–Chinese relations nor did it redound to the disadvantage of congressional candidates who received campaign contributions from this source.[7] But only in a very few types of bilateral relationships would governments risk such activity. Interference involving the use of overt lobbyists is not commonly utilized by governments of states in the first and second power categories, but it is utilized extensively by governments of less affluent states.

5. For example, Thomas E. Dewey came under the provisions of the Foreign Agents Registration Act when he was legal advisor for the government of Turkey shortly after retiring as governor of New York. See Senator Sparkman's remarks on this subject: U.S., Congress, Senate, Foreign Relations Committee, *Hearings, Foreign Agents Registration Act Amendments,* 88th Cong., 1st Sess., November 19, 20, 21, 1963.

6. U.S., Congress, Senate, Foreign Relations Committee, *Hearings, Activities of Nondiplomatic Representatives of Foreign Principals in the United States,* 88th Cong., 1st Sess., 1963.

7. For an example see Douglass Cater, "Senator Styles Bridges and His Far Flung Constituents," *The Reporter,* Vol. 11 (July 20, 1954), pp. 8–21.

A seventh type of interference is the use of subversion to achieve desired policy ends. The difference between this variety and the use of lobbying techniques is that the latter is overt, the former covert. In both cases individuals are seeking to influence policy in a desired direction, but in the case of subversion the individual conceals his foreign sponsorship. That sponsorship may be suspected, however. In some relationships, in fact, subversion is tolerated to a surprising degree, and where this is true the individual agent may actually spread the rumor that he is speaking for a foreign government.

Closely related but even less likely to be tolerated is the use of subversion to achieve desired personnel changes. If such activity is successful in producing high-level personnel changes, of course, policy toward the interfering government is likely to be altered, but not in the direction of hostility. Although the reactions of those leaders and segments of the public that did not wish to see these changes will certainly be hostile if the interfering government's role is understood, this hostility may very well not lead to an unfavorable alteration of policy toward the interfering power. On the contrary, those who suffered from the interference frequently will devote considerable energy toward persuading the interfering power to change its policy and give them support. This form of interference, however, becomes extremely risky when high-level officials are the targets, and an attempted personnel change that becomes known and fails can easily lead to a policy alteration in a hostile direction.

A ninth form of interference is the use of espionage for the purpose of reducing, or of gaining the means to reduce, a target state's capabilities. Activities here range from efforts to undermine morale to acts of physical destruction. Finally, there is the direct use of force to alter policies or personnel or to prevent their being altered by internal forces in a direction judged to be deleterious. It is this category which incorporates most of the acts classified as illegal intervention.

PATTERNS OF TOLERANCE OF INTERFERENCE
IN VARIOUS RELATIONSHIPS

The ranges of tolerance of interference vary widely for different governments and peoples. In the final section of this chapter some of the factors that generally determine the extent of tolerance will be explored. But the range is not by itself a sensitive guide for predicting the types and degrees of interference that will be permitted in a particular relationship. For example the government of state A may be regarded as having a broad range of tolerance of interference generally and that of state B a narrow one. Yet in their bilateral dealings with the government of state C, B may tolerate interference of more varieties and to a greater degree in most varieties than will A. If A has the same type of relationship with D as B has with C, however, A can be expected to tolerate from D a greater degree of interference within each variety than B tolerates from C. A may also tolerate more varieties of interference from D than does B from C. An estimate of the tolerance to be expected in a particular relationship therefore calls for an understanding of the general range of tolerance of each of the two actors plus the nature of their relationship.

The aspects of the relationship that are necessary to an understanding of the tolerance of interference are the following three:

1) *Relative power potential.* One factor that has a bearing on the range and degree of tolerance of interference in a bilateral relationship is the perceived power potential rating of each of the states. If two states are in the same or adjoining power potential categories, tolerance for interference will usually be lower than it would be in the same type of relationship if the two states had widely different power potential ratings.

Despite its obvious importance and the great amount of attention given it by scholars, the concept of a state's power potential remains unrefined. Authorities typically look upon power potential as the sum of a group of physical and nonphysical power factors. Morgenthau, for example, lists geography, natural resources, industrial capacity, military preparedness, population, national character, national morale, and quality of government. Real power as distinguished from power potential, Morgenthau argues, involves the exercising of influence. Whether a state's power base is utilized to its full potential depends therefore on the quality of its diplomacy.[8]

The difficulty in refining this concept is obvious. Whereas estimates of the natural resources and industrial capacity of a state may be generally accepted, evaluations of the power implications of the morale of a people are likely to vary widely. Even if a magic device for measuring the power quotient of factors such as morale and national character were discovered, the analytical utility of the discovery would be questionable. The perception by one state's government and people of the power potential of their state as compared with that of a second state is the analytically important unknown. Whether a people considers its state in a power category superior to, equal to, or inferior to the position of another state will significantly influence the bilateral relations of these states. The analytical goal to be sought in a refinement of this concept, therefore, is the ability to place states in power categories that conform to the modal perceptions of the politically influential element of a given people. Needless to say, the people of every state would not place the same states in the same categories.

No attempt at refinement of this concept will be made here. In the following chapter a scheme will be advanced for assessing the real power of states at a particular moment. With regard to power potential, however, states will be arbitrarily assigned to a numerical position in a descending scale.

2) *Type and intensity of relationship: allied, neutral, hostile, dependent.* The profile of a state's range and degree of tolerance of

8. Hans Morgenthau, *Politics Among Nations*, 3d ed. (New York, 1960), p. 139.

interference from another state will vary sharply depending on the type and intensity of the relationship it shares with that state. Intensity is indicated by such factors as the extent of communication, the number and variety of transactions involving the two states, and the size of the embassy staffs. The typology of relationships listed above is gross and unrefined; within each of the categories will be a wide variety of relationships and the boundaries between categories will be indistinct. Where intensity of relationship is very low interference outside normal diplomatic channels is unlikely, so no point is served by seeking to determine the range of interference likely to be tolerated. In this study the bilateral relationships of states will be categorized according to types that are assumed to coincide with what the two states perceive their relationship to be.

3) *Historical relationship.* A people's judgment of the power potential of its state relative to that of a second state, and its idea of the type of relationship that exists between the governments of the two states, will determine to a large extent the level of their mutual tolerance of interference. But a people's expectation of another government's behavior will inevitably be colored by the type of historical relationship that has existed between the two states. Indeed, the historical relationship may affect the perception and estimate of power potential and type of relationship. Therefore, estimates of the level of tolerance of interference that do not consider historical relationships are likely to be in serious error.

In the pages that follow, patterns of tolerance of interference will be suggested for five relationship variable combinations. These patterns are advanced tentatively, as they must be until they are tested in a number of carefully researched case studies.

Relationship one. Close allies in the same or adjoining power potential categories will have in their bilateral relations a relatively narrow range of tolerance of interference. If the government and people of one state believe theirs to be the more powerful, they are likely to have a broader range of tolerance of interference than will the government and people of a state who believe theirs is the less powerful.

Since close allies will presumably have agreed upon pursuing common goals, a frank and vigorous use of diplomatic channels to influence each other's policies can be anticipated. Discussions can be expected to include any aspect of their respective domestic affairs that has clear relevance to the pursuit of the common objectives. Interpretations as to what subjects do have relevance may be expected to vary, however, and the diplomat who stretches the definition too far risks being censured. Generally the less powerful of the two states is likely to be more sensitive. But the historical relations of the two states also influences sensitivity. The fact that the De Gaulle government in exile in World War II could not deal with the United States government on the same terms of equality as did the British government may explain France's greater postwar sensitivity to and narrower tolerance of interference from the United States through diplomatic discussions.

It would seem natural to assume that the more sensitive a state is to interference the less tolerant it would be. However, this assumption is misleading. In some relationships, one of which (the Iranian-American) will be described later, acute sensitivity to interference and a broad range of tolerance of interference are found together. But sensitivity to interference will affect the style and the profile of tolerated interference even though it need not affect the overall range of tolerance. For example, a highly sensitive government may have a relatively narrow view of the scope of permissible subjects for diplomatic discussions, but it may tolerate broad interferences in the form of strings attached to economic aid.

The second type of interference that is generally acceptable among close allies in the same or adjoining power potential categories is the use of educational and information channels. The American State Department, for example, may encourage and support an extensive speaking tour by a retired British diplomat even though it is well understood that this man is seeking to create a generally favorable climate of opinion for British foreign policy aims. Likewise, British diplomats seeking to explain British policy and thereby indirectly to influence American policy have easy access to American legislators and other nondiplomatic dignitaries. American journalists see nothing wrong in establishing close relations with British press officers even though quite obviously the latter seek to influence American policy through these contacts. Because of historical relations, Great Britain's ability to interfere in the United States in this manner probably goes further than that of any other nation. But any close allies generally will be granted far greater latitude in educational and propaganda activities than will neutral or hostile states.

Beyond these two types of interference, however, the degree of tolerance is narrow. Generally speaking, the governments and peoples of the western democracies understand that critical comments in the press of one state regarding the policies of the government of a second are not officially inspired and therefore do not constitute an official effort to interfere. Such articles may have some policy impact but if they are not perceived to have been designed to influence policy they will not meet the terms of the definition of "interference" as used here. In this event they are most unlikely to elicit a reaction so hostile as to affect adversely the relations of the two states.

Similarly, statements made by opposition leaders will commonly not be thought of as official interference and will not generate a hostile response. However, statements made by officials who do play a direct role in the foreign policy decision-making process are not viewed with the same easy tolerance. Any statement that appears to be intended to go over the heads of the public officials of a close ally will certainly be deeply resented and may well result in an alteration of the relationship. Even those statements which are meant to reinforce a government's position must be carefully phrased so as not to appear to constitute an attempt to support that government against its opposition.

If one or both of the allies is authoritarian or totalitarian the degree of tolerance in this category will be substantially narrower. An article appearing in a newspaper or a statement made by a nondiplomatic official of an authoritarian state will be assumed to represent official policy and therefore will have an impact only slightly less strong than would a statement by a diplomatic official. An authoritarian ally of a democratic state may well react strongly to a critical article appearing in a newspaper in the democratic state. The perception of the authoritarian leaders is likely to be colored by their knowledge of how the press is controlled in their own state. On the other hand critical statements made by diplomatic officials of a democratic state referring to the policy of an authoritarian ally are unlikely to evoke as strong a reaction as would comparable statements regarding the policy of a democratic ally. But the distinction is more apparent than real. If the ability to reach each other's public were comparable, the degree of tolerance of interference might be comparable. The key variables here are the availability of communications channels and the receptivity of the target public. In World War II, for example, American and Soviet officials could make harshly critical statements of each other's policies, but the American statements could not reach the Soviet people and the Soviet remarks fell on deaf ears in the United States. If the American government had broadcast its statements into the Soviet Union, Russia's tolerance may well have been considerably less.

Circumstantial evidence indicates that Soviet interference of this variety in the affairs of Communist China had a good deal to do with the speed and timing of the breakdown of the Sino-Soviet alliance. This suggests that the behavioral patterns in tolerance of interference for communist states do not differ substantially from those of noncommunist states.

Tolerance of interference in the category of attempts through public statements to influence the internal position of allied officials is quite narrow. Here again, when the allies concerned are the western democracies, the press and nongovernmental opinion leaders are expected to make critical evaluations of allied leaders' performances. There is likely to be more restraint, however, in evaluating allied leaders than in evaluating allied domestic policies. The American publications such as the *New York Times* that are widely read abroad usually are discrete in such evaluations. There appears to be an assumption that endorsing one group or another in an ally's national election would be unethical. In fact, the critical tenor of the *Times's* editorial remarks suggests an intuitive assessment by the editors of the limits of tolerance of the people whose leaders or policies are being evaluated.

Statements of approval or disapproval of particular allied leaders by officials who play a role in foreign policy must be very carefully and blandly phrased to remain within the limits of tolerance. An open endorsement of a particular party in an allied election campaign would almost certainly affect adversely the relations of the two states, even were the endorsed party to win. However, there is a wide variation in style and degree of tolerance of an ally's indicating a preference for one party or another in an election campaign. Generally speaking, the weaker ally will be more sensitive to interference but this sensitivity manifests itself more in the style of interference than in the degree. For example, an indication from a high American official that the United States preferred the Con-

9. For example in May, 1959, Hugh Gaitskill pounced upon a *Christian Science Monitor* report that Washington would seek a Conservative victory in Great Britain (*The New York Times,* May 4, 1959, p. 4).

servative Party in a British election could well help bring about a
Labor victory [9] and produce a deterioration in relations. A similar
expression of preference by a British official for the Democratic
Party in an American election would probably elicit little more than
a mild reaction in the United States and would affect relations very
little.

In the 1964 election Democratic campaign managers used to
their advantage the European press's clear preference for the Democrats and the privately expressed but publicly reported preference of
many leading European statesmen for the Democrats.[10] Since an
alliance is likely to be relatively more important to the weaker than
to the stronger state, however, politicians of the weaker state often
seek to demonstrate a superior ability to work with their stronger
ally. This gives the stronger state an opportunity to interfere in an
election as long as stylistic restrictions are observed. Whether by
design or not, the visit of President Eisenhower to England in
1959 just before the calling of an election granted Harold Macmillan the opportunity to demonstrate his close relations with the
American president.[11] And John Foster Dulles came close to openly
endorsing the C.D.U. in the first two West German elections.[12] So
anxious were the Germans for American support that this near
endorsement, far from boomeranging, was viewed as helpful by the
C.D.U. In 1961 when Vice-President Johnson visited Berlin during
the German election campaign, Konrad Adenauer reacted angrily
to Johnson's failure to take him along on his visit to Willy Brandt's
city. The obvious C.D.U. fear was that Johnson's trip could be
interpreted at best as a withdrawal of American support for the
C.D.U. and possibly even as a pro-S.D.P. gesture.[13]

Close allies in the same or adjoining power potential categories

10. *The New York Times,* November 2, 1964, p. 28.
11. *Ibid.,* September 1, 1959, p. 1.
12. *Ibid.,* September 4, 1953, p. 1.
13. *Ibid.,* August 23, 1961, p. 3.

are unlikely to employ as lobbyists citizens of the target state. If this is done at all the objective is likely to be a modest policy alteration; to go further would risk a strongly adverse reaction.

Similarly, close allies in this category are most unlikely to engage in subversion to alter each other's policies or personnel. A revelation that such an ally had engaged in subversive activities could produce a reaction strong enough to wreck the alliance. The same would be true of espionage—activities which in any case would be pointless if the alliance were a serious one. Only if the alliance were understood to be an ad hoc one resulting from a severe and common challenge would interference in these categories be tolerated. Thus a revelation during World War II that the Soviet Union was engaged in subversive activities against the United States would not have produced the same internal reaction that a similar revelation regarding Britain would have.

Relationship two. Close allies in widely differing power potential categories will have a relatively broad range of tolerance of interference. The weaker ally will inevitably be the more sensitive to such interference, a phenomenon explained in part by the greater effectiveness of the interference by the stronger. Many attempts by the weaker to interfere in the stronger's policies will be so little noted that no general reaction will follow. Commonly the weaker ally will not only note each such effort on the part of the stronger ally but also may interpret many innocent acts as attempts to interfere. There will, however, be some effective interference carried out by the weaker, which will be tolerated by the stronger ally.

A preliminary comparison of close allies in widely differing power potential categories with close allies in the same or adjoining power potential categories suggests that the degree of tolerance of all types of interference will tend to be greater in the former. Compare, for example, the Alliance for Progress program and the Marshall Plan. The ultimate political purpose behind these two programs was essentially the same, i.e., to create politically stable noncommunist regimes. Yet, despite a more manifest sensitivity to interference from the United States in Latin America than in Europe, the strings attached to the Alliance for Progress program are clearly visible. Had similar strings been attached to the Marshall Plan, our more powerful European allies would surely have refused to participate.

Since post-World War II diplomatic correspondence will not be available for scrutiny for many years, evidence is lacking to test the conclusion that also the degree of frankness in discussions will be greater between states whose power potential is unequal. Occasionally some evidence of this does come to the surface. Lincoln Gordon, when he was the American ambassador to Brazil, sometimes stated publicly what one can assume was even more strongly expressed privately. Following the ouster of the Goulart government by military coup d'état, for example, Gordon was quoted lecturing an assemblage of high-ranking Brazilian officers as if they were schoolboys.[14]

Certainly the educational and propagandizing techniques tolerated in this relationship category can go far beyond those tolerated in the previous category. The Fulbright committee hearings on the efforts of the Trujillo regime to influence American policy give ample proof of this point.[15] In the process of exploring the activities of an American public relations firm under contract to the Dominican government, the committee uncovered a highly ambitious program to influence American opinion, American policy, and even American personnel changes. The activities of this firm ranged through the interference categories of educating and propagandizing, lobbying to change policy, and lobbying for personnel changes. The line dividing overt lobbying from subversion is indistinct and a classification of many of this firm's efforts as subversion would not

14. *Ibid.,* May 6, 1964, p. 3.
15. "Activities of Nondiplomatic Representatives of Foreign Principals in the United States," pt. 6, June 14, 1963.

be unreasonable. What also emerges from the testimony in this case is the overall ineffectiveness of the program. As suggested above, part of the explanation for the surprising degree of tolerance for these activities by the government, by cooperating publishers, and by other involved citizens may be that those aware of these activities sensed how ineffective and basically unimportant they were. Still, in sum, this firm did help construct an image of General Trujillo in the United States that made difficult the task of those seeking to alter American policy in a direction unfavorable to Trujillo.

The converse of this picture can also be seen in American–Dominican Republic relations. Following the assassination of Trujillo and the ensuing struggle for power, the United States government became increasingly active in the Dominican Republic. Direct pressure was applied and reached its extreme form in the presence of marine-laden transports within easy view of the capital city. Overt American activity went so far as to leave no question in anyone's mind that Juan Bosch was Kennedy's choice for the presidency. Covert activity on behalf of this change has of course not been revealed, but obviously it was intensive and involved what could reasonably be described as subversion.[16] If this activity had gone beyond the Dominican people's tolerance of United States interference, surely they would have manifested their resentment in hostility toward the chosen instrument of United States policy, Juan Bosch. But there is very little evidence to indicate that the rightist opponents of Bosch made this a major issue. Obviously they were displeased with the direction of United States interference but not with American interference per se. On the contrary, they furnish an example of a group interfered against whose response was to seek an alteration of American policy to provide interference in their favor. These efforts met with obvious success in April, 1965. Bosch's leftist opponents, who could not conceivably

16. See for example *The New York Times,* January 20, 1962, p. 4.

ever be the beneficiaries of American support, did accuse him of being an American puppet. The overall ineffectiveness of such a line, however, argues that even this very extensive interference was within the limits of Dominican tolerance.

With regard to the category of interference involving public statements or expressions outside the diplomatic channels, the conclusion can be drawn with some confidence that the greater ally will have a broader tolerance. There is less evidence to indicate that the weaker ally is similarly tolerant. In 1961 President Ayub Khan of Pakistan addressed a joint session of Congress and levied a harshly worded attack on major aspects of American foreign policy, especially with regard to foreign aid.[17] By any definition the speech constituted a crude and obvious attempt to interfere, yet it was warmly applauded by the congressmen. One can easily imagine the frigidity with which a similar speech by President de Gaulle or Prime Minister Macmillan would have been received. Nor would President Kennedy conceivably have made such a speech in Karachi. Were one to make a collection of Ambassador Lincoln Gordon's public remarks in Brazil, the conclusion might be drawn that the greater ally can be as unrestrained as the lesser ally in public statements. But Mr. Gordon seems to be an exception.

Although a thorough study would have to be made before this conclusion could be drawn, a surface comparison of American newspaper coverage of our lesser allies and of our powerful allies seems to indicate a greater reluctance to criticize the former. If this observation is indeed accurate, much of the explanation could lie in the fact that journalistic coverage of our lesser allies is sporadic and superficial. But also it may indicate editors' reluctance to make critical analyses of a lesser ally because they sense that such analyses could be misinterpreted by the lesser ally and produce a hostile reaction. Prior to the overthrow in 1958 of our great friend Nuri as-Said of Iraq any number of Arabs must have told American

17. *Ibid.*, July 13, 1961, p. 5.

correspondents of their intense hatred for the Iraqi regime, but hardly a word to this effect was printed. Similarly, before the fall of Premier Menderes many Turks must have remarked on the dissatisfaction of intellectuals and military officers with the Menderes regime. Yet the collapse in 1960 of this supposedly solidly based government came as a complete surprise to newspaper readers. As further evidence of this point, the *New York Times* is still being accused of helping to bring down the Batista government in Cuba because of its interviews with Castro and the critical analyses of Batista's policies. Conversely, the conclusion can be drawn, with greater confidence, that the press of lesser allies has few such built-in restraints against criticizing the greater ally. This apparently can be done with impunity.

The interference category of espionage has no relevance in a discussion of close allies since presumably they would not wish to see each other weakened.

Before the next type of relationship, the dependent relationship, is discussed, the very broad range of tolerance of interference within each relationship type must be noted. Included within the type of close allies of widely differing power potential are, for example, the United States–Dominican Republic and the United States–Denmark relationships. Yet Denmark differs little from Great Britain in its tolerance of interference from the United States, whereas the Dominican Republic resembles states to be classified as essentially satellites of the United States. Brazil falls somewhere in the middle. The fact that Brazil stands well above Denmark in power potential suggests that a direct correlation of tolerance with estimated power potential cannot easily be made.

An important variable in determining the extent of tolerance of interference seems to be the degree of felt dependence. Since a very weak state is more likely to feel dependent than is a strong one, the weaker might be expected to be more tolerant of interference from a great ally. As will be discussed in the following section, tolerance is exceptionally broad where this felt dependence is so great that the relationship should be classified as a dependent one. Quite clearly, though, many other factors help determine a tolerance of interference. The historical relationship has been singled out as one intervening variable. In the concluding section of this chapter several other such factors will be discussed. But, in sum, a comparison of the extent of tolerance in the United States–Denmark relations with that in the United States–Dominican Republic relations illustrates the point stressed at the beginning of this section. Each government and people will have at any moment a general tolerance range of interference which may be classified as being broad, narrow, or intermediate. But the extent and type of interference tolerated will vary with each type of relationship. In this case the general tolerance range of the Dominican Republic appears to be exceptionally broad and that of Denmark exceptionally narrow. In their bilateral relationships with the United States the profile of tolerance should be similar but the degree should differ markedly.

Relationship three. A different pattern emerges for close allies if they are in widely separated power categories and if the two governments and most of the people of the weaker ally tend to believe that the weaker government could not survive internally without the support of the stronger. This relationship is referred to here as a dependent or satellite relationship. The range of tolerance of interference is broader in this relationship than in any other. There is much ambiguity in the definition of a dependent relationship, and the validity of placing particular states in this category vis-à-vis either the United States or the Soviet Union can certainly be challenged. Here the Soviet satellites are assumed to be Poland, Czechoslovakia, Hungary, Rumania, East Germany, and Bulgaria. Cuba is not included. The Soviet-Cuban relationship is assumed to fall into the previous category. American satellites are assumed to be Nationalist China, South Vietnam, Iran—and not long ago—

Laos, Jordan, South Korea, and Guatemala. Even the governments of Iran and Nationalist China by the mid-1960's had become borderline cases.

Most of the interference in a satellite relationship is direct and official. Both the American and Soviet governments will commonly have troop contingents operating in the satellites or such large military missions as to furnish the government significant support. Economic and technical aid on a massive scale are also solicited and freely granted. In addition there is less open but still obvious political, economic, and military support, such as the special forces which the C.I.A. supported to buoy up President Diem. Iranian Nationalists believe that comparable support is given the Iranian paratroopers, the one element of the military whose support the Shah can be confident of, and SAVAK, the Iranian security organization. But the United States has done nothing to compare with the Soviets' placing of Marshall Rokossovsky, a Soviet officer, as top man in the Polish security forces.

Obviously it would be a mistake to assert that the majority of the citizens of these states are happy about this aid. If they were happy with it their governments would not be classified as satellites. This is not the same, though, as saying that their tolerance of interference from their powerful ally has been exceeded. There is in each of the satellites listed above a certain percentage of the population who would wish to change the form of their relationship with the greater power from allied to hostile. For this element tolerance of interference from the greater power hardly exists. There are other elements who would retain the allied relationship or move to neutrality but would like to replace the government. Typically they will make the altering of the major ally's policy a primary objective. The conclusion therefore can be drawn that they are at least temporarily very tolerant of interference from their ally but would like to alter its form. The primary distinction between the American and the Soviet satellites in this regard is that the percentage of the population who would merely like to alter the form of interference, not eliminate it, appears to be much higher in the American satellites.

It is impossible to document satisfactorily a contention that in diplomatic confrontations the range of each other's domestic policies which the two allies seek to influence is very large, but there is some evidence that this is the case. Henry Cabot Lodge was apparently quite blunt in his discussions with President Diem and later explored in detail the policies of post-Diem regimes.[18] This is only to be expected since the powerful ally, which furnishes so much support, will feel it is entitled to an accounting. Soviet leaders apparently go into great detail in their policy discussions with satellite leaders.[19]

In the area of propagandizing, educating, and lobbying, a comparison with the Dominican Republic case discussed above would show that techniques and objectives were similar but that the two operations were far apart in elaborateness and effectiveness. Here the American collaborators could not have operated under the illusion of ineffectiveness. The Fulbright hearings disclosed that on the propaganda front no less a journal than the *New Leader* actually solicited financial support from registered agents of the Taipei government to help defray the expenses of an issue of that journal which was favorable to the Nationalist government.[20] According to a *Reporter* series, Chinese funds found their way into several election campaigns, including one of Richard Nixon's.[21] However, these disclosures apparently did not affect adversely the political fortunes of the recipients of those contributions. At its height the

18. *Newsweek,* November 4, 1963, p. 45.

19. For a description of these relations see Zbigniew Brzezinski, *The Soviet Bloc* (Cambridge, Mass., 1960).

20. "Activities of Nondiplomatic Representatives of Foreign Principals in the United States," pt. 7, pp. 723–26.

21. Charles Wertenbaker, "The China Lobby Part V, the Ubiquitous Major," *The Reporter,* Vol. 6 (April 15, 1952), pp. 20–24.

Kohlberg operation was quite an extensive one. Far from generating a hostile reaction, the activities of the China lobby blended with those of the McCarthy movement, producing the bizarre result that agents of a foreign power were able to stir serious doubts as to the patriotism of individual Americans and even of the liberal intellectual community in general. Just as in the Trujillo case, some of these operations were done on such a semicovert level as to be subject to the classification of subversion. According to Iranian Nationalist spokesmen, the Iranian government working through the firm of Kaston, Hilton, Chesley, Clifford, and Atherton is carrying on the same functions.[22] If this is true the excellent press the Shah has received in this country suggests these funds are well spent.

Comparable types of activities by satellites of the Soviet Union can hardly be expected. Public opinion and individual legislators would not be sensible targets for such activity. Attempts to influence Soviet policy and personnel which sought to work through intraparty factional disputes would be far more fruitful. Such activities of course would be difficult to document, and in any case they take on a different meaning since they occur within an assertedly international framework.

American interference has been best documented in the case of South Vietnam. Here it was revealed to embrace the same categories as used by the China lobby against the United States. Similar documentation is not available for Iran and Nationalist China although Iranian Nationalists and Formosans are only too willing to spell out the details as they see them. In the case of Iran tolerance of this activity is so great that many aspiring politicians find it advisable to gain the reputation of being "close to the Americans." [23] Furthermore the bitterly antiregime Nationalists have been

22. See for example *Daneshjoo* for June, 1964. The authority most frequently cited by the Iranians is Michael Parrish, "Iran: The Portrait of a U.S. Ally," *Minority of One,* December, 1962.

23. Richard W. Cottam, *Nationalism in Iran* (Pittsburgh, Pa., 1964).

preoccupied since the overthrow of Dr. Mossadeq with attempts to persuade the United States to interfere in their favor.

Few developments have been so revealing of the role of the press in American foreign policy as was the extensive and unfavorable coverage given the Diem regime in the spring and summer of 1963. President Diem and, even more, his sister-in-law, Madame Nhu, made clear their great annoyance. But remarkably enough David Halberstam and the other primary offenders were not expelled from the country. The contention could be supported, in fact, that our own people were less tolerant of this activity than was the South Vietnam regime. After Diem's overthrow Senator Thomas Dodd conducted a campaign using articles mainly by Marguerite Higgins to suggest that this press coverage was not only in error but damaging to the national interest.[24] This of course raises a question quite different from that being investigated here. Senator Dodd in effect was arguing that the American press should be extremely cautious in its criticism of an ally such as South Vietnam, but not out of fear of a hostile reaction from the criticized ally. Rather he feared the effect on American policy that might be caused by the tarnishing of an ally's public image. This point is worth developing here because the restraint shown by our press in criticizing an ally may be more the result of a wish to avoid the charge of damaging our national security than the result of an estimate of the impact of the article on relationships with our ally. In any event, the critical reportage of South Vietnam in that brief period is the exception. Iran and Nationalist China have been accorded in general an extremely favorable press coverage.

With regard to public statements made outside diplomatic channels, the greater power is clearly the more circumspect. Since the range of interference tolerated by the weaker power is broad, this point is important mainly in demonstrating how sensitivity to interference influences the profile and style of interference. President

24. U.S., *Congressional Record,* 89th Cong., 2d Sess., January 7–16, 1964, pp. 329–40.

Kennedy's public suggestion that a change in South Vietnamese personnel might be in order was quite exceptional and was made only as part of a sharp tactical bargaining maneuver.

The weaker power has no such restraint on either front. Press attacks on United States policy and personnel in the controlled press of Iran, South Vietnam, and Nationalist China have been common. In the spring of 1958, for example, a concerted press campaign in Iran was launched against the American ambassador.[25] But American tolerance of this criticism and of this obvious attempt to pressure the government into removing the ambassador was such that no official note was taken of the campaign.

Similarly, officials (and their women) of those three states are quite capable of giving the United States a severe tongue lashing. Two recent Iranian premiers, for example, climaxed their resignation statements with severe criticisms of American policy, remarks that must have had the Shah's approval. But all such comments suffer by comparison with those of Madame Nhu. If there were any question of American tolerance of interference from a satellite power, she should have disposed of it. Her attacks were directed at officials and policies alike, and she was not dismissed as being colorful and entertaining but essentially harmless. California Republicans demonstrated their appreciation of her possible utility in the 1964 presidential campaign by helping pay her hotel expenses.[26] Just as in the case of the China lobby, American politicians were ready to accept the aid of a satellite in combating their domestic political competition. Madame Chiang Kai-shek has been less dramatic but no less acceptable on similar occasions, and there is little reason to doubt that the Empress of Iran could do the same were American support for her husband to falter. It is difficult to

25. See issues of *Tehran Mosavar* during the spring of 1958 for the most pointed articles.

26. *The New York Times,* November 6, 1963, p. 17; November 14, 1963, p. 3.

imagine an English, German, or French lady, be she ever so attractive and charming, having a comparable effect.

Here again parallels are not to be found with the Soviet Union and its satellites. The fact that public opinion plays so minor a role in their policies precludes similarities. However, similarities could be found in the relations of France with some African states.

Relationship four. States with a neutral relationship will have a relatively narrow range of tolerance of interference. This appears to be true regardless of the difference in their power potential, although the weaker power is likely to be more sensitive to interference.

Diplomatic interchange between states with a neutral relationship is likely to be correct and to avoid attempting to exert influence on policy matters not of direct and immediate concern. Economic, technical, and even military aid may be granted by one government to another with which it has a neutral relationship. But the recipient government is certain to be wary of any strings that might be attached. When technicians are sent they are likely to be watched carefully to prevent their engaging in any subversion. Still the aid is given for the purpose of influencing the internal developments of the recipient state in a certain direction, and the recipient government may accept the aid if it believes the aid will help in the achievement of certain desired objectives. The results anticipated by the donor and the recipient may not be the same. But the recipient is likely to have evaluated the donor's motivations and to have concluded that either the donor's objectives are not likely to be achieved or that their achievement is desirable. In any case, the aid does constitute interference as defined in this study but an interference that neutral governments often tolerate. Some neutral governments, such as Burma, have on occasion rejected aid even though there were no obvious strings attached and the aid could have been used to further the government's stated objectives.

Tolerance of the use of educational and propaganda techniques to influence the public opinion of the target government is narrower in a neutral relationship than in any allied one. Whereas the State Department might actively help allied representatives in their efforts to reach the American public, Congress, and officials, there is likely to be little help granted the neutral representative for those purposes. Likewise it is difficult to imagine a public relations firm in the employ of, say, Yugoslavia or even India finding as easy access to publishers as those working for the Dominican Republic and Nationalist China. Similarly, editors in neutral states will be far less likely to publish a United States Information Agency news release than will their counterparts in allied states.

Public statements made outside diplomatic channels but which are interpreted as reflecting governmental policy will be less tolerated in this type of relationship. Compare for example the American reaction to the Ayub Khan speech mentioned above with that to the various statements regarding American policy made by India's Krishna Menon. An objective observer would have difficulty determining which man had made the more offensive remarks, implicitly and explicitly, but the general American reaction was favorable to the one but exceedingly hostile to the other. Similarly, statements by Vice-President Richard Nixon and Secretary of State John Foster Dulles that were critical of those governments which followed a nonaligned policy produced strong denunciations in the Indian press. When Secretary Dulles decided to withdraw the American offer for financing Egypt's Aswan Dam, he made a statement that was widely believed in the Middle East to be the first step in an interference campaign whose objective was the removal of President Gamal Abdul Nasser.[27] The reaction to the statement seems to have been more responsible for the violent Egyptian response than was the withdrawal of the financial offer.

Relationship five. One consequence of the decreasing likelihood that any thermonuclear power will resort to total warfare to resolve a conflict is that the profile of the tolerance of interference from

27. *Ibid.*, July 21, 1956, pp. 1, 3.

hostile powers has changed. In a relationship between hostile states a broad degree of interference is tolerated in some categories and very little in others. For nonnuclear powers in a hostile relationship, for example Israel and the United Arab Republic, there exists a tolerance profile more in line with pre-World War II patterns. Since there is at least a fair possibility that conventional warfare between them would not lead to nuclear escalation, they have the option of resorting to all-out warfare to resolve a conflict. A particularly offensive act of interference might therefore lead to armed hostilities. A similar act carried out by one nuclear power against another would be tolerated and would not lead to an altering of their relationship. But even in the U.A.R.–Israeli case, the likelihood of a greater power's intervening to contain the conflict has altered the profile.

The realization is gradually gaining ground that in this era of interdependence the diplomatic acts of one great power can substantially influence the internal developments of the other. For example should the Chinese Communists conclude that a highly nationalistic administration in Washington would give inadvertent assistance in their struggle with Moscow moderates, they could conceivably help produce such an administration in an election year. By creating serious difficulties for American policy in Southeast Asia and by urging communist parties elsewhere to take a hard line, the Chinese could add to the nationalistic appeal of an American candidate. Conversely, the Soviets by following a line of accommodation in our election year could reduce the appeal of the nationalistic candidate.

Although the election year opportunities for influencing Soviet policy are lacking, American and allied strategists can adopt similar tactics. The liberalization trend in the Soviet Union, spelled out in leadership terms, amounts over the long run to establishing in top positions men who grant increasingly high priorities to consumer goals and who are willing to see curbs on individual freedom of action whittled away. Implicit in this trend is an assumption that the Soviet Union is secure from foreign attack. Communist, chiefly Chinese, opponents of this trend argue that Soviet leaders misunderstand the absolute nature of western hostility to communism and, at the same time, overestimate the strength of the West. Since their actions affect the credibility of this perception, American foreign policy makers can strengthen or weaken the liberalization trend by the policies they follow. A very belligerent American stance coupled with a reduction in defense spending and a weakening of relations with American allies would seem to be the blueprint for weakening the liberalization trend since it would confirm the hard-liner's perception. Conversely, an accommodationist stance coupled with a maintenance of security preparations at a high level and a continuance of close relations with American allies would seem to be the blueprint for strengthening the liberalization trend since it confirms the perceptions of the more liberal leaders. Khrushchev's almost gleeful remark following the Soviet retreat from Cuba in October, 1962, that the paper tiger has atomic teeth could well reflect this intracommunist perceptual difference.

The conclusion to be drawn here is that a government in a hostile relationship, through its own overt policy, can influence the strength and direction of trends in an opponent state. Individual leaders may understand and seek to counter the impact of these policies but the system itself tolerates this form of interference, which is indirect and barely visible. This therefore is a case of implicit tolerance.

Examples of explicit tolerance in this relationship are not difficult to find. Possibly the best was referred to earlier: the granting of credits to the Polish Gomulka regime. Because of the American system of government the Poles cannot have any doubt as to the purpose of these loans. Since congressional approval is necessary, the State Department has been compelled to admit that the loans are meant to encourage Polish independence of Moscow and the internal liberalization trend. Quite clearly both Warsaw and Moscow are willing to tolerate this obvious effort to interfere. One can only assume that in Moscow the consequences of the loans are seen differently.

In direct diplomatic dealings the United Nations furnishes some indication of the style of diplomacy that will be tolerated and also of the breadth of matters of domestic concern that will be considered. In both cases the hostile relationship presents extremes. Vituperative oral exchanges can be made with the confident expectation that relations will not be affected. But both governments will interpret very broadly what constitutes policies of primarily domestic concern and will not participate in negotiations regarding these matters. The subject matter deemed suitable for discussion will be more narrowly defined in this relationship than in any other.

Tolerance for educational and propagandizing activities by agents of one government among the people of another state is in an inverse proportion to the intensity of hostility. With relaxation of tensions cultural and educational exchange programs are likely to build up momentum even though the opportunities for influencing publics are enhanced. But if hostility is intense, as with the United States–Chinese Communist relationship, interchange is close to zero. Needless to say, tolerance of interference in this category is lower in hostile relationships than in any other.

With regard to public statements and journalistic articles, there are few holds barred in this relationship. Violent attacks in the press and by leaders launched against both policies and personnel of the other government can be made with no serious policy consequences. Here too, however, there is a significant variation of the degree of tolerance from case to case. Tolerance of these acts is directly proportional to the intensity of hostility. Were the American press and government officials to make the same variety of critical remarks regarding Soviet policies and leaders in the 1960's that they made, say, during the Berlin crisis of 1948, an adverse Soviet policy reaction and possibly even a weakening of their liberalization trend could be expected.

To understand the difference in degrees of tolerance for lobbying, the reader should try to imagine the success of a Communist China lobby as compared to the spectacular achievements of the Nationalist China lobby. Obviously no candidate for office would be caught in the same neighborhood with anyone trying to give him a campaign contribution from Chinese Communist funds, and no publisher would consider the gift of a beautifully written and illustrated article picturing Communist China in glowing terms. Any American who would agree to take a position for the Chinese Communists similar to Kohlberg's would instantly find himself without influence and with very few friends. Nor would a Soviet lobby have much more success. Chinese Communist or Soviet tolerance for an American lobby would be equally slight.

On the other hand, hostile governments will expect and tolerate to a broad degree efforts to use subversion to alter policy and personnel. Here again the degree of tolerance increases directly with the intensity of hostility. Another Alger Hiss case in the mid-1960's could very well produce a deterioration in United States–Soviet relations. But a similar case involving the Chinese Communists would probably have little effect. Even here, however, other factors enter in. Hostility to Castro and Mao Tse-tung are probably comparable on the official level in the United States, but the American public is more fascinated by Castro. Were a high-placed American official discovered to be working for Castro, a major policy alteration in a hostile direction might well be demanded and take place. Geographical proximity and historical relations make the difference.

Similarly, espionage is expected and in the intensely hostile relationship even gross acts of espionage are unlikely to result in a change of relationship. But there are limits. The U-2 case may be an excellent one to demonstrate this point. It is clear enough that U-2's had been used for some time prior to the 1960 fiasco. Following the Camp David meetings, however, there had been a thaw in Soviet-American relations. Premier Khrushchev may have felt that acts of espionage such as the U-2 flights were not in keeping with the reduction of hostility between the two great powers. The excellent reporting of Thomas Ross and David Wise in *The U-2 Affair*[28] certainly leads to the conclusion that Premier Khrushchev was genuinely bewildered and chagrined at the Summit Conference, a stance that argues not at all for the conclusion that the U-2 incident was used only as an excuse. There is certainly little question that similar flights by Soviet planes over the United States at that time would have led to a deterioration of relations.

INDICATORS OF TOLERANCE OF INTERFERENCE

In the preceding section the contention was made that the range of tolerance of interference of two states will vary depending on their relative power potential, the type and intensity of their relationship, and their historical relationship. Far less emphasis was given to the historical relationship variable than to the other two, however. The purpose of this section is to try to explain some of the reasons for the wide variation in the range of tolerance of states which have similar relations and similar power potential differentials. To do so several indicators that have been identified will be examined. It will become clear that several of these indicators involve the historical relationship of states, but neither here nor in the previous section is there a comprehensive correlation of historical relationships with the range of tolerance of interference. This could be done only after a large number of case studies had been made.

Indicator one. The first indicator is the extent of consensus among a people. Where there are such deep and fundamental divisions among a people that a reconciliation of differences is difficult, the

28. Thomas Ross and David Wise, *The U-2 Affair* (New York, 1962).

soliciting of support from foreign governments by one or more of the competing factions becomes a real possibility. Where divisions are far less deep and a reconciliation of differences is feasible, a soliciting of foreign support would be far less likely, even unthinkable. The conclusion seems almost self-evident that both the breadth of tolerance and the sensitivity to interference vary in inverse proportion to the extent of consensus.

Post-World War II France is a case in point. Under the Fourth Republic the divisions that had characterized the previous republic persisted. Although these divisions were responsible for the political instability in France, they were not severe enough to cause competing factions to turn abroad for support. In the early Fifth Republic, however, despite great support for De Gaulle, dissatisfaction was so intense among the military and the nationalistic right that the possibility of soliciting foreign support was obviously perceived in France to be a real one. A visit to Washington by French rightist politicians in 1960 was viewed with great suspicion. After the abortive military coup d'état a few months later, a rumor was published and widely believed that the C.I.A. had a role in the attempted coup. With the total defeat of this military-rightist faction France appeared more united than ever before and far less tolerant of anything that smacked of foreign interference.

The extent of consensus, of course, is only a general indicator of tolerance of interference. Most of the more specific indicators that follow will be in fact refinements of this general point. Breakdowns of consensus, however, occur for a great many reasons that cannot be anticipated and therefore, as general as it is, the extent of consensus must be included as the first of the primary indicators.

Indicator two. The breadth of the range of tolerance varies inversely with the percentage of the population who are politically articulate. Earlier in this chapter reference was made to the fact that prior to the French Revolution blatant interference in the affairs of other governments was common procedure. But the

French Revolution was one of the first manifestations of the mass-politics era, a characteristic feature of which is the broad acceptance of nationalism. And, as nationalism spreads among the people, acts of interference that once were tolerated will cause a state to alter its relationship with another. Many of the new states of the world are only now entering the era of mass politics. Yesterday their political lives were dominated by small oligarchies, which tolerated interference very much as did their eighteenth-century European counterparts. But today comparable interference is not tolerated. A similar conclusion can be drawn for the modernizing intelligentsia as for the oligarchy. Although this group is almost always strongly nationalistic it will also be likely to adhere to such universal value systems as liberal democracy or socialism. Quite frequently in order to achieve the broader objectives this intellectual elite will solicit foreign assistance in its struggle with traditional and oligarchic forces and will not regard its actions as in any way unpatriotic. But this is true only in the early stages of political awakening. As political awareness extends further into the population, nationalism finds ready comprehension and acceptance, but such complicated values as those incorporated in what is meant by liberalism and socialism are less easily understood. By the time a substantial section of the public is politically aware, therefore, political leaders will be less willing to incur the risk to their reputations for patriotic purity by looking to foreign intervention to advance a domestic cause.

Indicator three. The appearance of a charismatic leader will produce conflicting degrees of tolerance of interference in different sections of the population. For those who fall under the spell of this leader, tolerance of interference declines rapidly. But for the opposition tolerance increases to the point that solicitations of foreign aid are not uncommon. A characteristic feature of this situation is a polarization of attitudes toward the great leader. For those in opposition, antagonism is likely to be all the more fierce since the possibilities of eliminating such a leader are slight. Thus the anti-Castro Cubans must turn to the previously much-maligned Yankee imperialist for support; President Nasser's Arab opponents look to the Anglo-American forces they have so long denounced; and opponents of President Sukarno are willing to request support from allies of the ousted Dutch. Should the charismatic leader achieve overwhelming support from the population, tolerance of interference would decline precipitously.

Indicator four. The breadth of the range of tolerance increases directly with the intensity of class antagonisms. This hypothesis is an adjunct to the first one regarding the relation of consensus and tolerance of interference. It is also partly dealt with in the second, which correlates tolerance of interference with the growth in political awareness, and with the sixth, which correlates tolerance of interference with colonial experience. But class antagonisms so frequently result in a broad tolerance of interference in the newly independent states that they deserve special mention. Typically, class conflict in these states involves a confrontation between the advocates of predominantly traditional values and the advocates of predominantly modern values. The latter group almost invariably preempts for itself the appellation "nationalist." Since the traditionalists will commonly have had a long record of dealings with the colonial or semicolonial power, and since these practices will have continued into the mass-politics era, a serious questioning of their patriotism will have occurred. Yet if the class conflict is severe enough, the modernizing group, calling itself nationalistic, may actually solicit foreign interference that does not differ in essence from that solicited by the traditionalists. The traditionalists, in turn, will regard those acts by the nationalists as intolerable and bordering on treason. Each of the warring factions, therefore, will be broadly tolerant of interference but will have a self-image of patriotic opposition to interference.

Indicator five. Decisive military defeat suffered by a people increases radically their tolerance of interference from new allies who formerly were enemies instrumental in administering the defeat. Thus Vichy France tolerated a very broad German interference but very little interference from Great Britain and the United States. In Vichy-controlled Syria in 1941, for example, open German interference was tolerated, but when the British insisted on removal of German influence the French resisted with surprising vigor. Postwar West Germany, Italy, and Japan all tolerated American interference and the East German regime was equally tolerant of Soviet interference. But the tolerance range for Soviet interference in West Germany, Italy, and Japan was very low, and the East German regime was no more receptive to American interference. Apparently the leaders of a successor government, ideologically attuned to one or more of the formerly enemy regimes, will be willing to tolerate a considerable amount of interference from the new allies in the interests of cementing new relationships. There seems to be nothing implicit in defeat per se that adds to a tolerance of interference. Post-World War II France, which had been thoroughly defeated, manifested a quite narrow range of tolerance of interference from her liberating allies.

As would be expected, this tolerance fades as the memory of defeat fades. West Germany was tolerant of American interference in their elections of 1953 and 1957, but in 1961 the Kennedy administration took considerable pains to avoid appearing to interfere. As mentioned above, this annoyed Konrad Adenauer at the time, but the decision was probably wise. By 1961 interference of the same order as that conducted by John Foster Dulles in the 1950's could well have produced a hostile reaction from the voters. By 1965 American neutrality in the German election paralleled that of American neutrality in the British election of 1966.

Indicator six. The people of a state which has recently emerged from a period of indirect colonial or semicolonial rule will have a relatively broad tolerance of and a relatively intense sensitivity to interference. This is particularly true if the colonial administration has exercised control through the traditional elements of the colonial society. Any people which has recently achieved independence will be hypersensitive to interference. But those who have endured indirect control will have a greater tolerance than those who have been under direct rule. When the colonial authorities relinquish control to popular leaders of a modernizing and anticolonial movement, the break between the colonial period and independence is clear-cut. The subject people are able to witness the lowering of the colonial power's flag, the departure of colonial officials, and their replacement by leaders who frequently have demonstrated their devotion to independence by suffering periods of incarceration. When control is relinquished to men who have worked long and well with the colonial administration the break is far less clear-cut. The flag is lowered but the native government which has cooperated closely with colonial officials remains in power and the colonial power's ambassador seems to take the place of the old governor general. For such people foreign interference in domestic political affairs will have had a long history and will be accepted as normal. In all likelihood opponents of the colonial-sponsored government will have tried to persuade the colonial administration to drop its support of the existing government and, failing this, will have looked into the possibility of assistance from a third country. After independence such behavior will continue. Sensitivity to and denunciations of interference will be that much greater if the competition can be described as traditional vs. modernist, but soliciting of foreign assistance also will be more energetic.

When a people of a theoretically independent state believe their government to have been in fact the creature of a colonial power, sensitivity to and tolerance of interference will be, if anything, even greater than that described above. Here too political leaders will accept as one of the political facts of life the necessity to gain the approval of an external power. Therefore, even though such behavior is a far cry from that of people in a genuinely independent state, soliciting foreign assistance will be tolerated. Several of the Caribbean republics fell into this category in the recent past, and the Trujillo government of the Dominican Republic, for example, was widely believed to be indebted to the United States. When the Kennedy administration openly interfered against the Trujillos, liberal modernizing elements in the Dominican Republic happily cooperated, and their counterparts throughout Latin America applauded even the gun-boat diplomacy aspects of that interference.

Indicator seven. When a people and/or government of a state believe their continued independence is threatened by an external force, they will tolerate substantial interference from the government of a state that can furnish them protection and is either ideologically compatible or is believed not to have designs on the subject state's independence. Examples can be found most readily among those states which have lived in the shadow of a greater one. Middle Easterners, historically threatened by both Britain and Russia, had a very broad tolerance for German interference through World War II. Similarly, under Castro, Cuba's broad tolerance of interference from the Soviet Union is directly related to the perceived threat from the United States. A substantial case could be made, in fact, for the contention that the Soviet presence in Cuba is likely to persist as long as United States policy is intransigently hostile to the Castro regime. Were there to be a thaw in Cuban-American relations, Cuban tolerance of Soviet interference might well narrow.

Some readers may have concluded that the use of the term "interference" in this chapter has been unwise. Since "interference" was defined in terms of "influence" why not substitute the more neutral "influence" for "interference"? The term "interference" inevitably generates an emotional response and this in turn affects the persuasiveness of the analysis.

This line of reasoning has its temptations. No one who is striving for analytical objectivity wants to use a term that will imply certain values to the reader. Yet in this case the suggestions that a substitute be found for interference is somewhat analogous to arguing that Kinsey should have found a euphemism for the term "sex." The purpose here is to gain an understanding of interference and to reduce the normative confusion surrounding the term. Therefore to avoid using the term would be self-defeating.

Basically, the reason for the pejorative connotation of "interference" is the disparity between theory and practice. It is an inherent assumption of the nation-state era that each nation state should be master of its own house. In practice there have always been severe limitations on the freedom of action of the government of a nation state, even with regard to what its people believe to be matters of domestic concern. Most of these limitations fall into anticipated patterns and go unnoticed. Only the aberrant action is widely noticed and condemned as unwarranted interference.

A basic assumption of this study is that since World War II a trend away from the autonomous nation state has gained such force that, despite temporary hinderances such as that caused by Gaullist France, the interaction patterns of states are being fundamentally altered. One manifestation of this change is a much greater concern with altering policies and developmental trends of other states. The surface evidence of this heightened concern is a substantial quantitative increase in what people perceive to be interference. Despite this quantitative increase, however, acts of interference are still being judged by pre-World War II standards and hence condemned. If the assumption is correct that diplomacy in this era will involve a far greater concern with the domestic affairs of other states, this wholesale condemnation of interference per se can actually work against the achievement of generally desired ends. What is called for instead is an evaluation of acts of interference from the point of view of the end being sought and of the means being utilized to achieve that end.

Interference has been defined in this chapter in such a way as to embrace all acts by a government and people designed to limit the freedom of action of the government and people of a target state. The concept of the range of tolerance of interference was advanced to provide a means for identifying what acts will not be tolerated and will generate a hostile response from a target government and/or people. These are the acts that generally are referred to in popular usage as "interference." If the American adherent of the liberal democratic ideology should evaluate various acts of interference, he is likely to favor proscribing some varieties as ideologically offensive. He should likewise give careful attention to those acts of interference which go beyond a people's tolerance threshold to ascertain that the desired end warrants such activity. But he is unlikely to do either if the normative confusion which envelops the concept of interference persists.

From the first pages of this study the point has been made that a predominant characteristic of American diplomacy is its ad hoc style. In speculating about the reasons for this style it is too easy and too pessimistic to blame it on immutable national character. A central hypothesis here is that the deep confusion regarding interference that is found in the attentive public, and the foreign policy governmental elite as well, is a primary obstacle to overcoming this style. Any well-developed, long-term strategy will involve the use of tactics that by pre-World War II standards would be classified as ethically questionable interference. But by post-World War II standards few of these tactics need go beyond the range of tolerance of interference.

2 | POWER IN TERMS OF LEVERAGE

FEW SCHOLARS in any field have had more of an impact than Hans J. Morgenthau has had in international relations. His focus on power as a means, and national interest defined in terms of power as an end, have convinced some, annoyed many, and attracted the attention of the entire field. But in the past several years the spotlight has been moving steadily away from Morgenthau, and in the more recent theoretical approaches the remarkable fact is that so little has been built upon the foundation he has laid.

This study accepts the analytical utility of a focus on power in the study of world politics. In fact, the impact Morgenthau has had on the field is probably a reflection of the usefulness of this focus, but he was not successful in refining this concept. His gross power factor list is reasonable,[1] and his contention that a summation of these power factors gives only a picture of power potential and that a realization of power depends on the quality of diplomacy indicates the direction in which further refinement is necessary. Unfortunately, however, at this point Morgenthau takes a side track that is fully as diverting as is his view of power as an end. His

1. Hans Morgenthau, *Politics Among Nations,* 3d ed. (New York, 1960), pp. 110–48.

answer to the question of what quality of diplomacy is necessary is really a return to the great, intuitive diplomat comparable to the ideal picture of some of those of the eighteenth and nineteenth centuries.[2]

The analytical inadequacy of this conclusion can be seen by viewing the relations of the United States and Nationalist China. If Morgenthau's power factors are used to examine the power differential, the conclusion is obvious that this is a relationship involving a great power and a minor power. If confronted with the apparent fact that despite this power differential Chiang Kai-shek is very influential in the determination of American policy in the Far East, Morgenthau must point his finger at a deficiency in the quality of American diplomacy. This would not be very helpful, nor is it really accurate if taken literally. The point here is that a sum of physical and nonphysical power factors does not give an accurate picture of the power differential of two states at any particular moment. Or, to state the same conclusion in other words, the power potential picture tells very little in any instant in time of the relative ability of a government to influence the policy of another government.

What the United States–Nationalist China relationship illustrates is that real power—the ability to influence the policies of other governments—is at any moment largely the product of strategic interactions. The very significant influence Nationalist China is able to exert is a consequence of strategic interaction between great powers. Because of American strategic decisions the island of Formosa is a focal point in the Cold War conflict. Were American strategists to decide tomorrow that the military significance of the island has been exaggerated and that on the political front an effort should be made to establish formal diplomatic relations with the Communist Chinese, the real power of Nationalist China would decline immediately.

2. *Ibid.*, pp. 560–64.

But a dramatic alteration in real power as a result of a change in strategy of one national actor is exceptional. In this case the real power of the Nationalist Chinese is vicariously based on American power potential. Therefore an alteration of American strategy could have an instantaneous and drastic effect. No such rapid alteration in the real power of Communist China could follow from a strategic decision of the American government or of any other government. A serious alteration of Communist China's ability to influence could be accomplished only by an elaborate, multifaceted American strategy involving many other states and designed specifically to reduce the power potential of Communist China. The really solid claim of Communist China to first-category power rating is not based on physical power factors such as natural resources and industrial capacity; rather, the nonphysical power factor of image is the most important source of their influence. A strategy designed to alter this image is therefore probably the one most likely to produce a reasonably rapid decline in Chinese ability to influence.

A sum of the vital physical and nonphysical power potential factors is clearly basic to the total power picture. Such a summation will permit the categorizing of states with regard to their power potential. In order to understand the role played in world politics by any particular government, the analyst must know the relative power potential of that state. In particular he must understand which states should be placed in the first power category because these states will be the primary actors in world politics. Interaction of primary states in turn becomes a central factor for determining the power positions of all the other actors at any particular instant in time. The assumption cannot be made that a state's real power at any moment will correspond to the power potential category in which it has been placed. In fact, only those states that are placed in the first power potential category are likely to exercise corresponding real power.

What this adds up to is a conclusion that the power picture of a state at any time consists of a summation of the power potential factors plus the consequences of strategic interaction. Theoretical studies in the field of international relations concerned with power have tended to focus on analytical refinements of the power potential factors or on negotiating or bargaining theory, in which the basic power picture is a given. The Sprouts, for example, have made considerable progress in refining power potential factors,[3] and Kenneth Boulding has pointed the way for an investigation of the frequently neglected concept of image.[4] Those such as George Liska and Fred Iklé, who have focused on negotiations, have thus far limited their approach mainly to systematic abstractions of historical rules of behavior.[5] As such their studies have not gone far beyond being negotiating recipes to be used when a current situation parallels an historical situation in which the abstracted rules were successfully applied. Bargaining theory emanating from game theory, of which Thomas Schelling furnishes the best example,[6] does offer some general bargaining rules which have an obvious power relevance. But this approach is even less easily related to a general strategic picture since the game situation, even the n-person, non-zero-sum game in which mixed motives and imperfect communications are assumed, cannot be an isomorph of that picture. Far too few situational variables can be incorporated.

Relating strategic interaction to the power picture is done only tangentially. The closest to a direct approach to this task is to be found in George Modelski's *A Theory of Foreign Policy*.[7] Some of Modelski's external power factors are in fact results of strategic

3. Harold and Margaret Sprout, *Foundations of International Politics* (Princeton, N. J., 1962).

4. Kenneth E. Boulding, *The Image* (Ann Arbor, Mich., 1956).

5. Fred Charles Iklé, *How Nations Negotiate* (New York, 1964); George Liska, *The New Statecraft* (Chicago, 1960), *Nations in Alliance* (Baltimore, Md., 1962).

6. Thomas Schelling, *The Strategy of Conflict* (Cambridge, Mass., 1960), *Arms and Influence* (New Haven, Conn., 1966).

7. George Modelski, *A Theory of Foreign Policy* (New York, 1962), Ch. 2.

interaction. Others, however, are aspects of the power potential factors of image and military preparedness. Modelski's overall view of power approximates that of a zero-sum situation and this view leads him away from strategic interaction to more concrete and measurable aspects of the basic power picture.

The purpose of this chapter is to explore the potential of the ancient concept of leverage as an analytical device for explaining the power implications of strategic interaction. Leverage as a concept has been intuitively understood and utilized throughout man's history, but a systematic study of leverage as an analytical device in interstate relations has never been made. Indeed, the term is rarely defined. As used in this study, leverage refers to those means not involving direct action by which one government can exercise some influence over the policies of another government at any particular time. The analytical assumption to be tested is that the power implications of strategic interaction can be discovered by constructing the operative system of levers in a diplomatic situation. In this study only bilateral relations will be considered and the leverage systems explored will be those operating between two states at a particular moment. However, such systems will always incorporate levers that are outgrowths of the broader relations of the two states.

A first step in approaching the problem of constructing leverage systems is to develop a fairly inclusive typology of levers that are utilized in interstate relations. This can be done by studying a wide variety of strategic situations and attempting to abstract from them the operative lever types. Any such endeavor quickly reveals that levers fall into two general categories. The levers in one are active and manipulatable, those of the other passive and far less manipulatable. When applying levers of the first category, a government will be attempting to compel another to follow a certain, usually specific, course of action by promising a reward that can be withheld or by threatening to carry out some damaging action. When applying levers of the second category, a government will be attempting to persuade another to follow a certain, usually general, course of action by pointing out that if it does so developments favorable to the target government will occur or that if it does not developments deleterious to the target government will occur. In the leverage system the passive levers can be thought of as independent variables, the active as dependent.

It is important to note from the outset that leverage analysis is of little direct use in determining goals. Certainly the gaining of a leverage advantage over a target government should not in itself be an end. What leverage analysis has to offer the strategist is a means for assessing feasibility. The goals of a foreign policy are clearly determined before a strategy is developed for achieving these goals. In developing strategy, however, the leverage system should be of considerable value and indirectly should influence the determination of goals. Leverage analysis may indicate that a government lacks the ability to achieve certain goals or that goals must be modified if they are to be attainable.

The leverage system that operates between two or more states will always be a unique system. But certain regular patterns can be identified and much can be learned from observing both the regular patterns and deviations from these patterns. The leverage system will of course vary a great deal depending on the environmental relationship of the states under consideration. Those environmental variables which are considered here to be most important are the following: (1) intensity of involvement (great, medium, or slight); (2) type of relationship (allied, neutral, hostile, dependent); (3) power potential category (one through five); (4) tolerance range of interference (broad, medium, narrow); (5) political leaders' attitudes toward world power configuration (essentially status quo, essentially anti-status quo, strongly anti-status quo).

A suggested typology of levers is the following:

I. Passive levers
   A. Perceived public attitudes
   B. Perceived possibility of great power involvement
   C. Awareness of interdependence
      1. For defense
      2. For economic prosperity
      3. For the achievement of other strategic objectives
   D. Perceived long-range alterations in power potential ratings
   E. Perceived economic and/or political instability
   F. Perceived possibility of adverse effect on personal friendships of top negotiators or national figures
   G. Perceived irrationality, irresponsibility, or instability of leadership
   H. Perceived likelihood of accidental war
II. Active levers
   A. Perceived ability to grant or withhold economic, technical, and/or military aid
   B. Perceived ability to influence actions of a third country
   C. Perceived possible willingness to resort to war
      1. Thermonuclear
      2. Limited nuclear
      3. General conventional
      4. Limited conventional
   D. Perceived trade opportunities
   E. Perceived vulnerability to exploitation of domestic political dissatisfaction
   F. Perceived transnational appeal of an ideology
   G. Perceived willingness to alter the type of relationship

In order for the utility of this analytical approach to be explored fully, case studies should be made of relationships involving a large number of possible combinations of the environmental relationship variables. Here only two types of relationships will be considered, the dependent and the neutral. In each case the intensity of involvement will be great but there will be considerable variety in the combinations of the other three variables.

DEPENDENT RELATIONSHIP: UNITED STATES–IRAN

The environmental relationship picture here is as follows:

1) Intensity of involvement great

2) Close allies, in which the government of one state (Iran) is perceived to be dependent on the government of the other (U.S.) for its continued existence

3) First-category power (U.S.) and fourth-category power (Iran)

4) Range of tolerance of interference broad (Iran) and narrow (U.S.)

5) Dominant political leadership of both states essentially status quo

Passive Levers

The passive leverage system in operation is as follows:

Awareness of interdependence for defense. An allied relationship by definition is one in which there is an awareness of interdependence for the achievement of basic strategic objectives. Each ally will be in a position to remind the other that it must adhere generally to a given set of norms of behavior or risk an alteration of the allied relationship. If awareness of interdependence is strong, this risk will not be taken lightly. The resulting lever is to be classified as passive since basic strategies are not easily altered. In the leverage system operating between two allies, awareness of interdependence is likely to be the most important lever in determining patterns of interactions.

The advantage in this lever type should logically lie with the government that is less intensely aware of interdependence. Normally this will be the government of the state with the greater power potential. In the case of United States–Iran relations the Iranian regime is clearly the more intensely aware of interdependence. Both Americans and Iranians believe Iran's position outside the Soviet orbit is a result of American containment strategy. Since this strategy has been seriously criticized with regard to Central and South Asia, the contention being that containment in this area constitutes overcommitment, there is a possibility that American strategy could be changed to exclude the defense of Iran. Consequently any Iranian regime that fears Soviet domination is likely to look to the United States for support and to be acutely aware of the danger of strategy change by the United States government. But for the regime of the Shah this is doubly significant. The assumption here is that the very survival of the Shah's government depends on a continued American belief that his government is essential to United States security interests. The most dangerous opponents of the Shah are the Nationalists, followers of the late Premier Mohammad Mossadeq, who are philosophically pro-West but who would undoubtedly pursue a neutral foreign policy. A substantial case could be made for the proposition that United States interests would be better served by a neutral, noncommunist, and popular Iranian regime than by an outspokenly anticommunist regime that is so unpopular with the middle-class and intellectual elements as to increase the receptivity for a popular front with the communists. Since the Shah's government is aware of this potential alternative, the leverage advantage for the United States is considerable.

This American advantage should not be viewed in isolation, however. The virtue of systems analysis lies in its recognition of complex interactions, and the government of the Shah has a series of powerful levers, to be discussed below, which can be used in its relations with the United States. One of these, paradoxically, is that of a perceived willingness to alter the type of relationship and this is an active lever. A view of the leverage system as a whole will be necessary to understand why the United States should have an advantage with the passive relationship lever and Iran with the active.

Perceived economic and political instability. Since the late 1940's American foreign policy has been essentially that of containment. For Iran as for other littoral states of the communist world this policy has been developed through a strategy of encouraging the establishment of stable, noncommunist regimes that can withstand Soviet pressures. Since the mid-1950's American policy makers have made clear their belief that a stable noncommunist Iran can be achieved only by the Shah. So emphatic has been their public and private dedication to this belief that the potential leverage advantage mentioned above could not be developed. At the same time the unpopularity of the Shah with important segments of the politically aware population is recognized by these policy makers. As a result the Iranian government has, and fully understands it has, a very substantial leverage advantage. It can argue that there will be the most deleterious consequences if active support for the regime is discontinued or even reduced. The Shah's government thereby has been able not only to wrench economic, military, and technical assistance from the United States but also to demand, successfully, political assistance to strengthen the regime against the possibility of a Nationalist or popular front coup d'état. This open evidence of support for the regime and denial of any thought of turning a more benign eye on the Nationalists further reduces the American leverage advantage gained from Iran's awareness of interdependence.

Perceived irrationality and irresponsibility of leadership. The Nationalist opposition refers to the Shah and his allies as "suitcase patriots." By this they mean their bags are packed and their Swiss bank accounts are full. While this is, and is meant to be, political calumny, the Shah's past behavior lends credence to the belief that if a crisis should develop he and his lieutenants would flee the country. American officials cannot avoid being aware of this possibility since a favorite tactic of the Shah is to hint at abdication if American policy is less than pleasing to him.[8] As will be described below, the Shah has also been very adept at flirting publicly with the Soviets. Since American policy makers are known to believe there is no safe alternative to the Shah, the Shah is granted both an active and a passive lever. The passive lever permits him to call for a continuing and unwaveringly favorable attitude toward his regime since anything less than this might encourage thoughts of abdication.[9]

Perceived public attitudes. The case was developed above that perceived anti-Shah attitudes on the part of middle-sector Iranians paradoxically adds to the bargaining advantage of the Shah. The United States does have some leverage strength with regard to attitudes, however, which although very weak on the passive level is potentially strong on the active level. On the passive level American diplomats can point out to the Shah that real stability calls for a program of attracting middle-sector support and that economic programs will be insufficient unless they are complemented by political reform. Whereas this argument may have logical force, any political reforms that would attract the noncommunist opposition would weaken the immediate control of the Shah and the Shah is therefore almost certain to reject any such argument. The active lever aspect will be described below.

Perceived attitudes of the American public offer leverage opportunities for both Iran and the United States. But different American publics are involved. For that large section of the population below the attentive public which has a general awareness of United States

8. The Shah on a visit to the United States in 1962 referred to the onerous nature of "this king business" (*The New York Times,* April 14, 1962, p. 1). To officials who had listened to allusions to the possibility of abdicating, this remark was more ominous than cute.

9. The Shah's sensitivity on this point was demonstrated in 1957 when the opposition Iran Party made an open attempt to gain American favor (Richard W. Cottam, *Nationalism in Iran* [Pittsburgh, Pa., 1964], pp. 234–36).

foreign policy but lacks sophistication, the advantage is Iran's. Also for that section of the attentive public which is highly nationalistic the advantage is Iran's. Neither of these groups, however, could be described as avid supporters of the Shah. Indeed, below the attentive public and even within it, most Americans will have only the fuzziest notion of where Iran is. Yet were Iran to pass under a popular front rule, that country would suddenly become well known. Were it possible for the partisan opposition to accuse the administration of culpability in this calamity, Iran could become important in inter-party conflict. To preclude any such eventuality, the administration is likely to be cautious about undertaking a policy that would be described by its opponents as "rocking the boat." The Shah's aware-ness of the importance of this public attitude is demonstrated by the large expenditure he allegedly makes to an American public relations firm whose task is to solidify the image of a gracious, reformist, and militantly anticommunist leader.[10] The better estab-lished this image, the more reluctant the policy maker will be to consider backing any alternative Iranian political force.

However, more and more well-informed Americans are coming to the conclusion that the Shah's image is in sharp variance with reality. A number of critical books and articles have appeared and the activities of anti-Shah Iranian students have raised doubts in many minds. This presents obvious leverage possibilities for the United States. American diplomats could argue that, whereas the government has shown its devotion to the Shah's regime, any marked growth in skepticism regarding a policy of all-out support for the Shah, especially if such skepticism found its way into Congress, could cause difficulties. However, the argument could continue, such critics could easily be disarmed if the Shah were to take the kind of political measures, such as granting some freedom of political activity, that would expand his political base of support.

10. Michael Parrish, "Iran: The Portrait of a U.S. Ally," *Minority of One,* December, 1962.

But this potential leverage strength has never been developed by the American government. On the contrary, just as it was when President Diem began receiving such a vociferously bad press in the United States, the American government seems anxious to do what it can to modify the press attacks and to silence some of the Shah's critics.[11]

Active Levers

The active levers in operation are the following:

Perceived ability to grant or withhold economic, technical, and military aid. At first glance, and in spite of the elimination of most forms of economic aid, the substantial military aid still being granted Iran would appear to give the United States a strong leverage advantage. But, given the American strategic goal of doing everything possible to keep in power an anticommunist or at least noncommunist regime, this aid is likely to be continued. Iranian political leaders are fully aware that their country is regarded as strategically vital and that the aid will continue to be forthcoming as long as the regime is determined to resist Soviet aggression. Were a neutralist regime to come to power, the American objective would in all probability remain the same. Only if United States policy were to change drastically, such as to a reconsideration of a Fortress America strategy, would there suddenly be a major leverage advantage in offering aid. There will be, inevitably, disagreement regarding the level of aid needed to protect the Iranian regime from its internal and external enemies and to provide economic and political stability. Aid that is given beyond the level that is regarded by American officials as the minimum necessary for the achievement of these goals will grant leverage strength to the American government. For example, budgetary assistance pro-

11. For example in 1964 the American government took preliminary steps toward the expulsion of an outspoken Iranian student, Ali Fatemi, because of his opposition activities.

vided the Iranian government to help extricate it from avoidable financial difficulties can be made contingent on substantial budgetary and administrative reforms.

Perception of vulnerability to exploitation of domestic political dissatisfaction. As described above, the Iranian government has a passive leverage advantage in the perception of American public attitudes by American government officials. But this perception does not grant a corresponding active leverage advantage. American tolerance for interference, though generally narrow, is at its broadest in the Iranian case, and the Shah is deeply involved in an effort to influence American public attitudes. Regardless of the skill of his public relations representatives, however, the Shah has an insuperable obstacle to overcome—the American public's disinterest in, and ignorance of, Iran. Were the Iranian regime overthrown, public notice would be focused on the state, but this would be of little help to an ousted regime.

On the other hand, the United States has a strong potential leverage advantage here. Iran has a generally broad range of tolerance of interference and a particularly broad one with regard to American interference. This tolerance manifests itself, for example, in energetic efforts by the noncommunist opposition to the Shah to persuade the United States to transfer its support from the Shah to them. The Shah has made abundantly clear his concern that this maneuver might be successful,[12] and this concern could be the basis for some substantial leverage strength for the United States. Either directly or indirectly the Shah could be informed that full American backing was contingent on his carrying out political reforms. Needless to say, this leverage strength remains only potential.

Perceived willingness to alter the type of relationship. In December, 1959, the Iranian government executed a maneuver which illustrates a maximum utilization of an active lever of this type. At

12. See the Iran Party example, above (Cottam, *Nationalism in Iran*).

that time the Soviets were obviously led to believe that Iran was prepared to sign an agreement with them that would go a long way toward nullifying the Baghdad Pact (CENTO). Despite cries of anguish from his American, British, Turkish, and Pakistani allies, the Shah seemed determined to sign. At the very last instant and with a high-powered Soviet delegation already in Tehran the Shah reneged. In the process of this maneuver he wrenched from the United States a concession of unknown but probably substantial size in the form of military aid.[13] American officials could not be blamed for taking seriously the Shah's threat to sign, considering past demonstrations of what they would describe as irrational behavior. Yet Soviet annoyance at having been the goat in this affair was sufficient that there is not likely to be a repetition.

The Shah's threats to abdicate also amount indirectly to a threat to alter United States–Iranian relations. At least American officials view such an action as being a prelude to a neutralist or even popular front regime. When American diplomatic records of this era are available, they may well demonstrate that this was the Shah's most frequently used lever.

In Chapter Four this leverage system will be related to an ideal type of United States–Iranian relations. For purposes here the summation of this leverage system points clearly to the conclusion that there is a very substantial difference between the power potential ratings of the United States and Iran and of their relative abilities to influence each other's policy at a particular time. The advantage is Iran's, but it is obvious that this advantage will persist only so long as the preservation of the Iranian regime is believed to be a vital aspect of American foreign policy strategy. A further conclusion of this analysis is that in their relations Iran has made full utilization of its leverage potential but the United States has not. But superior Iranian diplomacy is not the explanation for this. To develop fully its potential leverage, fairly simple and obvious

13. *Ibid.*, pp. 239–41.

tactics were available to the Iranians. But for the United States the tactical requirements were not at all obvious and furthermore ran counter to the American diplomatic style.

DEPENDENT RELATIONSHIP:
UNITED STATES–NATIONALIST CHINA

The picture of the United States–Nationalist China environmental relationship, including their relative power potential ratings, is similar to that of the United States and Iran. A brief glance at this relationship is therefore in order to see if similar leverage system patterns manifest themselves. The United States–Iranian leverage system in outline was as follows:

I. Passive levers
- A. Awareness of interdependence for defense
- B. Perceived economic and political instability
- C. Perceived irrationality and irresponsibility of leadership
- D. Perceived public attitudes

II. Active levers
- A. Perceived ability to grant or withhold economic, technical, and military aid
- B. Perceived vulnerability to exploitation of domestic political dissatisfaction
- C. Perceived willingness to alter the type of relationship

The applicability of much of this leverage system to the United States–Nationalist China case is quickly obvious. But three basic environmental differences exist, two of which result in advantages for the Chinese and one for the United States. First, the really militant opposition in Nationalist China to the Chiang Kai-shek regime comes from the Taiwanese rather than the Chinese community. Since the entire Chinese community feels threatened, it has little choice other than to stand with Chiang. The regime is therefore less dependent for its continued existence on the United States than is the Shah. Second, the American public is far more aware of

China than of Iran and many still feel that mainland China's fall to communism could have been averted if the Democratic Truman administration had been wiser. Third, the possibility of a change in American strategy which downgrades the importance of the Nationalist Chinese is far more likely than one which ceases to regard a noncommunist Iran as strategically vital.

The broader base of support that exists for Chiang relative to that for the Shah reduces, as compared with Iran, the active leverage potential the United States possesses by virtue of its perceived ability to work with dissident domestic forces. Conversely, the Iranian passive leverage advantage resulting from the United States' awareness of Iran's political instability does not have an equal counterpart for China.

Although the Chinese gain here is slight, relative to Iran, it enjoys a great advantage due to the American public's interest in China (or interest as perceived by American politicians).[14] As the success of the China lobby demonstrates, the Chinese have been able to bring their case to the American people. Not only is the passive leverage advantage due to perceived public attitudes much greater for China than for Iran, but the Chinese also have an active leverage advantage because of the American politician's conviction that China can exploit American partisan politics. Furthermore, the Chinese have an additional passive leverage advantage because of the perceived possibility of an adverse effect on the personal friendships of national figures. Here the friendship for and feeling of obligation to Chiang on the part of prominent Americans is no small item in Chinese leverage advantage. The expectation that a tactical line

14. A recent survey would lead to a questioning of both public interest and public attitudes as generally assessed by political leaders. Of those interviewed, 39 per cent had never "heard of or knew" there was a Chinese Nationalist government on Taiwan; of 72 per cent who knew of the communist government on the mainland, 73 per cent favored discussing acute problems with that government (*The New York Times,* December 15, 1964, p. 9).

would be damaging to the friendships and sense of obligation to Chiang can result not only in the vetoing of such a line but even in a failure to comprehend its utility.

The Chinese passive leverage advantage resulting from the American perception of irresponsibility of leadership and active leverage advantage due to the American perception of a willingness to change the type of relationship are approximately equal to those of Iran. Chiang, like the Shah, in order to pressure the United States, has threatened in the past to give way before the mutual enemy.[15] Because of the perceived appeal of the Chinese Communist siren call to return with full honors to the motherland, many Chinese Nationalist leaders (but not Chiang) are in a position to exercise substantial active leverage.

However, the impact on the entire leverage system of the Chinese perception of the increasing possibility of a basic change in American strategy is a major one. France's establishing of diplomatic relations with Communist China, for example, adds to the real American power in its bilateral relations with Nationalist China since the Chinese understand that a basic altering of strategy is possible for the United States as it was for France. To the extent that the Chinese seriously believe a change in American strategy is likely there will be an adjustment in America's favor in every lever in the Chinese-American system. This could result in a significant reduction in the differential between the power ratings of the two states and the actual ability each has to influence the other's policy.

Similar analyses could be made of the former governments of Diem in South Vietnam, Syngman Rhee in Korea, Castillo Armas in Guatemala, and Boun Oum in Laos. An analysis of the United States–Jordan relations would be similar but would need to incorporate the added dimension of the United Kingdom–Jordan leverage system as well.

15. Joseph W. Stilwell, *The Stilwell Papers,* ed. T. H. White (New York, 1948), pp. 125–26.

DEPENDENT RELATIONSHIP: U.S.S.R.–EAST GERMANY

The popular myth that the so-called Soviet satellites are power-less in their dealings with the mother country has long been rejected by scholars of the area.[16] Yet there remains a good deal of confusion regarding the actual power relationships here. Certainly the emerging power picture here shows substantial differences from that of the United States and its dependent allies, but the resemblances are striking.

The Soviet–East German environmental relationship is as follows:

1) Intensity of involvement great

2) Close allies in which the government of one state (East Germany) is dependent for its continued existence on support from the government of the other state (U.S.S.R.)

3) First-category power (U.S.S.R.) and third-category power (East Germany)

4) Range of tolerance of interference narrow (U.S.S.R.) and broad (East Germany)

5) Dominant political leadership essentially anti-status quo (U.S.S.R.) and strongly anti-status quo (East Germany)

Passive Levers

The passive leverage system in operation is as follows:

Awareness of interdependence for defense and economic prosperity. Unlike the United States–Iranian case, there is an acute awareness of economic interdependence between the Soviet Union and East Germany. The latter is one of the major heavy industry areas of the Soviet bloc and therefore is of great importance to the economic prosperity of the entire area. Since the East German trade outlets to the West have been restricted, the East German economy

16. Zbigniew Brzezinski, *The Soviet Bloc* (Cambridge, Mass., 1960).

has been tied to that of the communist world in a way that could not now be altered easily. Otherwise the parallel with the United States–Iranian case is close. Since the very survival of the East German regime is dependent on Soviet support, including the presence of Soviet troops, the intensity of awareness of interdependence is greater for the East Germans than for the Soviets. Consequently the leverage advantage lies with the Soviet Union. Just as in the United States–Iranian case, an alternative strategy exists for the Soviet Union which could result in the withdrawal of all-out Soviet support. Because of the immense unpopularity of the East German regime, the danger of a revolt is omnipresent and a revolt in East Germany could easily produce an escalation into World War III. Therefore, East Germany stands as perhaps the strongest roadblock in the path of a Soviet accommodation with the West. Assuming that an accommodation with the West and the avoidance of World War III are Soviet objectives, it is possible that the temptation exists among some Soviet policy makers to find a face-saving device by which Germany could be reunited without too drastically upsetting established trade patterns. Certainly western statesmen have explored this possibility.[17] To the extent that the East German regime thinks any such change in strategy is possible, the Soviet leverage is strengthened.

Perceived economic and political instability. The passive leverage advantage held by East Germany because of Soviet perceptions of East German instability is closely comparable to the Iranian advantage over the United States. As long as the protection and perpetuation of the East German regime is a clear and unequivocal strategic goal of the Soviet Union, domestic political instability is

17. See, for example, the so-called "Herter Plan," which constituted an excellent probe of Soviet policies toward German questions (*The New York Times,* May 15, 1959, p. 12). This point has been explored thoroughly by Robert Beranek in "The 'Second' Berlin Crisis and the Foreign Ministers' Conference at Geneva (1959): A Case Study of Soviet Diplomacy." Unpublished Ph.D. dissertation, University of Pittsburgh, 1966.

the primary basis of East German leverage strength. The very unpopularity of the regime compels the Soviet Union to give all varieties of aid and full political support to it. The Berlin Wall may be symbolic of East Germany's failure to attract popular support, but it is also symbolic of the lengths to which the Soviet Union will go in its efforts to buoy up the East German regime.

Perceived irrationality and irresponsibility of leadership. Walter Ulbricht does not hold a position in East Germany comparable in importance to that of the Shah in Iran or Chiang Kai-shek in Nationalist China. A threat from him to fly to Peking is not likely to produce panic in Moscow, and he is most unlikely to be able to persuade his government to accompany him. Furthermore, he is in no position to shift his alliance. The West could not receive him and Peking could hardly give much aid. Here, though, it should be noted that Peking does seem to recognize some opportunity for bargaining.

There is one area in which the Soviets may fear what they could regard as irresponsibility from the East Germans. Whereas an accommodation with the West seems to have Soviet favor, the East German regime has much to fear from an accommodation that could result in a Soviet acceptance of German reunification. Therefore, were the East Germans left in full charge of the Berlin access routes, East German officials might well behave in a belligerent manner simply to counter a trend toward accommodation. Certainly any sign of Soviet softness here stirs Ulbricht into diplomatic action.[18] Soviet leaders may believe, therefore, that if East Ger-

18. An example of this and an excellent surface picture of the Soviet–East German power position can be found in the diplomatic maneuvers regarding Berlin immediately after the Cuban missile crisis. The Soviets obviously decided to modify their stand in Berlin as well as in Cuba. Ulbricht was compelled to withdraw a very belligerent statement during the crisis and then some weeks later backed down very far in his stand on Berlin. In the Communist Party Conference held in Berlin in January, 1963, Khrushchev used the occasion to make clear Soviet determination to preserve East German sovereignty despite the thaw in relations with the West (*The New York Times,* December 6, 1962, p. 1; January 7, 1963, p. 2).

many were left alone to regulate access routes it would act in an irresponsible manner. If the Soviets do perceive such a possibility the East Germans will gain leverage strength. In order to avoid giving the East Germans full control of access routes to Berlin the Soviets may well make other important policy concessions.

Perceived public attitudes. The great unpopularity of the East German regime, of which the Soviets have demonstrated their awareness, has already been described as the basis for the passive leverage strength of the East German regime. To this extent the East Germans parallel the Iranians. But there is no parallel of the American public in the Iranian case with the Soviet public in this case. Even with the liberalization trend, Soviet public attitudes can be pretty well disregarded in determining leverage strengths.

Active Levers

The active levers in this relationship are the following:

Perceived ability to grant or withhold economic, technical, and military aid. As was true in the United States–Iranian case, the Soviet Union's granting of very substantial and diverse aid does not result in its gaining much leverage advantage. This will be true as long as Soviet strategic objectives regarding East Germany remain unchanged. East German awareness of the Soviet determination to maintain the regime prevents the Soviets from arguing that aid will be cut off or reduced if a specific line is not followed. The only aid having significant leverage potential is that which East Germans believe the Soviet leaders regard as beyond the minimum necessary to maintain the regime.

Perception of vulnerability to exploitation of domestic political dissatisfaction. In the United States–Iranian case the point was made that the United States could conceivably turn to the leaders of the underground opposition to the Shah and yet not alter the basic objective of a stable, noncommunist Iran. No such alternative exists for the Soviet Union. Underground East German leaders would certainly shift sides in the Cold War if they were able to gain control. Therefore this potential leverage does not exist for the Soviet Union.

On the other hand, Soviet leaders have demonstrated a willingness to interfere in the personnel selections in eastern European countries and the East German leaders have no reason to question the likelihood that the Soviets would use any instrument of intrigue in East Germany. With Soviet troops and security officers present in large numbers in East Germany the means are at hand for physically removing undesired personnel. Yet the fact that the East German regime remains the most Stalinist of the so-called eastern European satellites could lead to a questioning of the Soviet ability to interfere.

The conclusion is not obvious that Ulbricht's longevity reflects a lack of Soviet power. To carry out a liberalization program requires a certain amount of popular acquiescence if not support. Ulbricht's unpopularity is in base probably more a reflection of a refusal of the East German people to accept communism and national division than a reaction to Ulbricht as a political personality or to his policies. A successor would probably be just as unpopular unless he inaugurated liberalizing measures and spoke in terms of possible reunification, and any such action might well produce an explosion just as it did in Hungary. Given the delicate state of East German stability, the Soviets would in any case probably be reluctant to risk stirring dissension within the East German leadership ranks. Soviet leverage in this category, therefore, does not compare with that of the United States in Iran.

Perceived willingness to alter the type of relationship. Chinese wooing of the Ulbricht government can be assumed to indicate the former's belief that East Germany could move in the direction of Communist China. But, as noted above, the Chinese could hardly replace the Soviets as perpetuators of the East German regime. Soviet troops are probably still essential. Any basic altering of the relationship is therefore ruled out. However, some leverage potential does exist for the East Germans in interstate communist conferences. Since Moscow obviously wishes to enlist the support of as many communist regimes and communist parties in noncommunist states as possible in the struggle with Peking, each of these regimes and parties is granted a leverage advantage for use against both Moscow and Peking. This is true of the East Germans. An ambiguous remark on some matter of contention between Peking and Moscow may compel the Soviets to follow a tough, China-like policy in Berlin.

Perception of the possibility of recourse to limited conventional war. Among the paradoxes of the dependent relationship, none is so striking as the fact that a resort to force is not ruled out. A characteristic feature of this relationship is a willingness of each of the two partners to so involve itself in the domestic affairs of the other as to come perilously close to meeting the definition requirement of clandestine political warfare. American behavior toward President Diem is a case in point. But the Soviets have demonstrated a willingness to go one step further and to turn to armed warfare to force an ally back into line. Having resorted to armed intervention once, the Soviets have established credibility for any threats, even unspoken ones, to do so again. And this credibility grants them an active leverage advantage in dealing with the eastern European states, although growing manifestations of Rumanian independence argue that this threat is losing force. In East Germany the presence of Soviet troops adds weight to this lever but, at the same time, the fear that a resort to force could result in expanded conflict reduces the leverage strength somewhat.

The summation of the U.S.S.R.–East German leverage system indicates that, as was true in the United States–Iranian case, there is a substantial difference between the power potential ratings of the Soviet Union and East Germany and of their relative abilities to influence each other's policies at any particular time. As was true in the United States–Iranian case, the East German advantage is totally dependent on the continuation of current Soviet strategy. An alteration in that strategy, however, would do more than reverse this differential. It would probably result in the elimination of the state.

Poland with its Rapacki Plan and East Germany with its tough stand on Berlin are, if surface appearances can be accepted, sharply opposed in their views of what communist foreign policy in Europe should be. That the Soviet Union in the final analysis stands closer to East Germany may be a reflection of the greater strength of East Germany's leverage position in intrabloc dealings. Paradoxically, the fact of Poland's greater political stability reduces her leverage advantage over the Soviet Union in comparison with that of East Germany. There is no great fear that if the Soviet Union is less than enthusiastic in its support of Polish foreign policy objectives a revolution might occur in Poland. On the other hand the intensity of awareness of interdependence is lower in Poland than in East Germany and this reduces somewhat the Soviet passive leverage advantage. This loss is more than offset, however, by the gains resulting from the greater stability of the Polish regime.

NEUTRAL RELATIONSHIP: UNITED STATES–INDIA

To test further the heuristic value of leverage analysis, three cases of a neutral relationship, each involving India, will be compared. The first leverage system to be described is that operating between the United States and India. The environmental relationship of this case is as follows:

1) Intensity of involvement great
2) A neutral relationship
3) First-category power (United States) and second-category power (India)
4) Tolerance range of interference narrow (United States) and medium (India)
5) Both essentially status quo powers

Passive Levers

The passive levers in operation are the following:

Awareness of interdependence for defense and economic prosperity. As will become clear in the pages that follow, India's real power position relative to that of the United States and most other states has declined with the intensification of the Sino-Soviet dispute and with the Chinese border attack against India. Prior to the Chinese invasion, the Indian government's perception of defense needs was very limited. No challenge from China or the Soviet Union was seriously anticipated. Pakistani aggression however was feared and the Indian government was compelled to spend far more than it wished on defense. Since Pakistan was an American ally, India could hardly be expected to depend very much on the United States for defense. On the contrary, India would have been much happier to see American military disengagement in the area.

The American government's view, on the other hand, was that the protection of the entire littoral area of the communist world was vital to American security. India, as potentially the greatest non-European littoral power, must inevitably play a stellar role in this battle. Furthermore, for many in the American government foreign policy community, India was a particularly attractive if unwilling ally since its vigorous economic development program utilized democratic methods and was therefore a democratic model which other developing lands could look to.[19] This latter picture of India was far from being universally held. For some members of Congress, in particular, India's socialism was anything but attractive,[20] and for congressmen, governmental officials, and members of the attentive public alike India's neutralism was annoying.[21]

19. Cecil V. Crabb, Jr., *The Elephant and the Grass* (New York, 1965), pp. 177–97.

20. U.S., *Congressional Record,* 82d Cong., 2d Sess., June 13, 1952, p. 7103.

21. Crabb, *The Elephant and the Grass,* pp. 169–76.

Nevertheless, the American awareness of interdependence for defense was much greater than India's awareness and therefore the Indians enjoyed a passive leverage advantage. In order not to weaken India's defense capabilities and in order not to drive India closer to the communist camp, American diplomats would take careful note of India's views of our South Asian policy.

This leverage advantage was reversed almost literally overnight when even Krishna Menon was compelled to agree that China was indeed a very serious threat to India's independence and economic well-being.[22] With this perception a dominant one, India's intensity of awareness of interdependence for defense became much stronger than that of the United States. South Asia is far away and for those old-fashioned but surprisingly numerous followers of Captain Mahan this is an area in which our commitments are already greater than our capabilities. Furthermore, weariness with the South Vietnamese war makes the proposal of a negotiated withdrawal from the area pleasing to many ears.[23] This very division of opinion as perceived by the Indians strengthens American leverage. India is now confronted with the problem of maintaining an American conviction that India must be defended. Therefore the Indian government is likely to be far more responsive to American views, domestic and international, than it was before the Chinese invasion.

With regard to awareness of interdependence for economic prosperity, the leverage advantage has always been with the United States. The success of India's economic plans is heavily contingent on outside aid, and the United States is obviously one of the two great potential donors. Prior to the Chinese border incursions, this American advantage was more than offset by the Indian advantage from the defense interdependence point. But since the Chinese attack the overall advantage is American.

22. *The New York Times,* October 21, 1962, p. 1.
23. Walter Lippmann, "Our Problem in Vietnam," *Newsweek,* September 28, 1964, p. 23.

Perceived economic and political instability. As long as American strategy regards a strong, independent, and economically viable India as essential to American security, American perceptions of economic and political instability in India grant India a passive leverage advantage. This lever parallels and complements the previously discussed one.

Perceived public attitudes. An almost implicit assumption of American political leaders and analysts alike has been that the greater the public consensus concerning a strategy the greater the strength of American policy. Certainly any administration would want to have sufficient backing for its general strategic objectives to be able to plan a policy with the confidence that it can be put into effect. But this study suggests that domestic challenges to strategic objectives can grant a passive leverage advantage. In the Iranian case the point was made that American public attitudes favorable to the Shah reduced American leverage and those unfavorable increased American leverage. A parallel point is obvious here. The greater the American awareness of a need for defending India and for helping make India's economic planning successful, the weaker is American leverage. Therefore an attack on the value of aid for India by a section of the American public can actually grant some power advantage.

Similarly, the growth in public awareness in India of the Chinese Communist threat has weakened the passive leverage strength of India. Now Indian leaders understand that they must build a proper defense on the Chinese border or suffer serious political consequences. Since any substantial defense improvements require aid from abroad, the Indian government must, and potential donors know it must, request military aid. The setbacks suffered by Indian communists also have the effect, at least temporarily, of reducing Indian leverage. Such changes in Indian attitudes may have the long-term consequence of altering American strategy in the direction of a firmer commitment to the defense and economic support of India. Should this occur, India's potential passive leverage strength would be relatively greater. This points once again to a previous conclusion that the leverage system is of only momentary validity and that leverage analysis has little direct bearing on normative questions.

Perceived long-range alternatives in power potential ratings. In the leverage system as a whole involving the United States and India, the American perception that India's power potential rating may well rise to the first category is an essential aspect. The potential passive leverage advantage is India's. Since India is likely to be of increasing importance in world affairs, American policy makers will feel more constrained in their dealings with India than they would if India were likely to decline. This is particularly true because of the earlier point that India can be a democratic model of rapid economic development for others to emulate.

Active Levers

The active levers at work in this case are as follows:

Perceived ability to grant or withhold economic, technical, and military aid. The potential active leverage advantage held by the United States here is significantly greater than it is in the United States–Iranian case. This is true even though both Iran and India are part of the littoral area of the communist world. The explanation for the difference here lies in a lesser intensity of American official and public awareness of interdependence and some serious public ideological misgivings. As a result, suggestions from American diplomats that aid might be reduced will be taken much more seriously by Indian than by Iranian leaders. Therefore the potential exists for demanding a substantial *quid pro quo* for the American aid.

Perception of vulnerability to exploitation of domestic political dissatisfaction. As described in the previous chapter, the neutral relationship is generally characterized by a narrow tolerance range of interference. Because of the lack of consensus in India, however, the range of India's tolerance of interference is broader than that of the United States. It is possible that American support would be solicited by and granted to certain party or factional leaders. Should the government fear this possibility, a potential active leverage advantage would rest with the United States. Any crass use by American diplomats of this Indian fear, such as a direct threat to give covert support to a rival faction, would be precluded because it crosses the tolerance threshold. But a more subtle threat could have the effect of persuading the Indian government to hew closer to a policy line desired by the United States.

Perceived ability to influence actions of a third country. Both the United States and India have potential active leverage strength of this type. Prior to the Chinese-Indian crisis the overall advantage clearly rested with the Indians, but this is no longer true. Occupying as it did a unique position of leadership in the neutral or non-aligned world, the Indian government was understood to have considerable influence in United States relations with many neutral governments. This granted India an advantageous leverage position. India could, in arguing for a specific United States policy line, add to the strength of its argument by promising a reward (improved United States–neutral relations) or making a threat of deleterious consequences (worsened United States–neutral relations). But the Chinese attack changed Indian attitudes, and the failure of neutral nations to come more positively to India's assistance reduced the credibility of Indian claims to have a determining influence with other neutrals.

Also, because Soviet strategy quite clearly called for close Soviet-Indian relations, the Indian attitude could be significant in determining the tenor of United States–Soviet relations and of specific Soviet policies toward the United States. Here again the Chinese attack on India reduced Indian leverage strength. Should the Sino-Soviet split become irreparable, however, this leverage advantage would probably be restored and possibly even strengthened.

The American leverage strength stemmed from a perceived American ability to influence Pakistani policy. Pakistan's awareness of interdependence with the United States for defense against India was intense but there was virtually no American awareness of interdependence with Pakistan for defense against India. American awareness of interdependence with Pakistan was with regard to the threat from the Soviet Union or China and here Pakistani awareness of interdependence with the United States was of only moderate intensity. This granted the United States an overall leverage advantage with Pakistan and, paradoxically, with India. The United States was in a strong enough position to veto an aggressive Pakistani policy against India and this was well recognized in India. Ironically the Chinese attack on India and the rapid and extensive American support of India destroyed the American leverage advantage with Pakistan and therefore with India. Pakistan no longer perceived an interdependence with the United States in the Indian-Pakistan struggle. On the contrary, the United States was now busily arming the Indian enemy. Instead Pakistan perceived an interdependence with China in their mutual struggle with India. This perception and the accommodation with China that followed resulted in a growing acuteness of American awareness of a communist threat to the Pakistani position on the communist littoral. Pakistan's diplomacy developed this potential leverage advantage to a remarkable degree.

NEUTRAL RELATIONSHIP: SOVIET UNION–INDIA

The environmental relationship picture here is as follows:
1) Intensity of involvement great
2) A neutral relationship

3) First-category power (U.S.S.R.) and a second-category power (India)

4) Tolerance range of interference narrow (U.S.S.R.) and medium (India)

5) Essentially status quo (India) and essentially anti-status quo (U.S.S.R)

Passive Levers

The passive leverage system in operation is as follows:

Perceived economic and political instability. Post-Stalinist Soviet strategy has obviously held Soviet-Indian friendship as a goal. At the same time Soviet spokesmen have never wavered in their proclamations of a devotion to the goal of a communist world. A logical conclusion from this is that friendship with democratic India is a tactical goal but that ultimately the Soviet Union wishes to see a change in the Indian government system. As such the Soviet Union is surely far less concerned with political and economic stability in India than is the United States. This conclusion is apparently less widely held in India than in the United States, but to the extent that it is held in India it grants the Soviet Union a passive leverage advantage. India's awareness of its own political and economic difficulties leads to a desire for outside aid, including Soviet. But since, unlike the United States, the Soviet Union will not have long-term stability as a goal, the Soviet leverage advantage is substantial. As the Sino-Soviet dispute worsens, the point may soon be reached at which an awareness of interdependence will exist with India and against China. At that point, the policy price that India would feel compelled to pay for Soviet aid would not be much higher than that for American aid.

Perceived public attitudes. Since the Soviet public is not considered to be a directly determining factor of any real significance in the formulation of Soviet foreign policy, Soviet public attitudes are of no concern here. Indian public attitudes are of concern and grant the Soviet Union a passive leverage advantage. Whereas Indian lack of consensus and receptivity for communism gave India leverage strength with the United States, they form the basis of Soviet leverage strength in the Soviet-Indian system. In the United States–Indian case, Indians could point out that an American failure to support India could bring about an Indian collapse which, in turn, would hurt American security. In the U.S.S.R.–Indian case, the Soviets can point out that a failure of India to follow a desired path could result in a loss of Soviet aid, which in turn, would add to divisive and procommunist attitudes in India. India's fear of China likewise adds to a popular desire for Soviet material and diplomatic support, and for this support the Soviets are in a position to ask a big price.

Perceived long-range alteration in power potential ratings. In explaining the high priority the Soviet Union grants to friendship with India, a reasonable assumption is that the probable rise in India's power potential rating is relevant. The same point holds true in the momentary leverage picture. Soviet belief that India may one day be in the first power potential category grants India passive leverage strength of significant importance. This Indian advantage would seem to be directly proportional to the intensity of Sino-Soviet rivalry.

Active Levers

The active levers are the following:

Perceived ability to grant or withhold economic, technical, and military aid. As the passive leverage system analysis suggests, the Soviet Union is granted a much stronger active leverage advantage here than is the United States. India clearly desires aid from both but the American objective of a strong, democratic India as compared to the Soviet objective of an eventual communist India makes for a stronger Soviet lever.

Perception of vulnerability to exploitation of domestic political dissatisfaction. As with the United States–Indian case, this lever gives the Soviet Union an advantage. India's ability to interfere directly in either American or Soviet affairs is very limited, but the converse is not true. The greater the internal divisions in India, the more susceptible India will be to interference. But the Soviet advantage here is greater than the American because of the ready-made instrument for interference that is the Communist Party of India. Also, the perceived greater willingness of the Soviet Union to engage in interference of this variety adds to the Soviet potential. Leverage exists to the extent that Indian leaders are convinced that the Soviets are refraining from or might be willing to refrain from making maximum use of the interference potential of the Communist Party of India.

Perceived ability to influence actions of a third country. Previous to the Chinese attack on India, both India and the Soviet Union had considerable leverage strength of this type. Since the Soviet Union has pursued for more than a decade an active policy of seeking friendly relations with neutrals, Soviet perceptions of Indian influence in the neutral world granted India leverage strength just as did the similar American perception. With the revelation of India's weakness in being unable to attract neutral support at the time of the Chinese attack, her strength was significantly reduced.

Soviet leverage here was due to India's perception of Soviet influence with the Chinese. This perception was altered sharply when the Soviets were shown to be unable to restrain the Chinese from attacking India. Worse still, they may not even have been informed of the attack. With the deepening of the Sino-Soviet crisis, Soviet leverage here steadily weakens.

Perceived transnational appeal of an ideology. The appeal of communism to important segments of the Indian public and the publics of neutral nations which have looked to India for leadership also gives the Soviets a leverage advantage. This lever exists to the extent that Indian leaders believe the Soviet Union is purposely refraining from making maximum use of this psychological warfare potential. That this is indeed a lever of some strength in other areas as well as India is demonstrated by the frequency with which other governments demand that the Soviets refrain from making inflammatory appeals to their publics.[24]

NEUTRAL RELATIONSHIP: COMMUNIST CHINA–INDIA

The relationship variable picture here is as follows:

1) Intensity of involvement great

2) A neutral relationship

3) Both second-category powers with China holding a higher position in that category.

4) Tolerance range of interference narrow (China) and medium (India)

5) Essentially status quo (India) and strongly anti-status quo (China)

Passive Levers

The passive leverage system in operation is the following:

Perceived public attitudes. The Chinese public is not perceived to have more than a very indirect influence on Chinese policy and therefore is of no concern here. Given apparent Chinese strategy, Indian public attitudes are of scarcely greater leverage concern. One of the results of the Chinese attack was a crystallization of anti-Chinese sentiment and a weakening of the appeal of communism, especially Chinese style. If this grants India a potential passive leverage advantage, Chinese actions would indicate the advantage is slight. Apparently the Chinese are little concerned with the growth of hostility toward them and the drift in Indian sentiment away from the doctrinally neutral.

Perceived long-range alterations in power potential rating. Both

24. For a discussion of Soviet problems here see Frederick C. Barghoorn, *Soviet Foreign Propaganda* (Princeton, N. J., 1964).

China and India are widely perceived to be likely to rise in power potential ratings. Generally such a perception will grant a potential passive leverage strength to the state which is expected to rise in relative power rating. This is true, however, only if long-range strategy calls for friendly relations with the rising power. In this case, China does gain some leverage strength because India clearly does wish to have friendly relations with China. On the other hand, given present strategic behavior, India gains no leverage strength. On the contrary, the Chinese, far from looking to friendly relations, seem determined to discredit India.

Perceived irrationality and irresponsibility of leadership. The image of Chinese leadership created in part by the Chinese attack on India is one of unpredictability. For China to launch an attack on the greatest of neutral states, the sponsor of Chinese Communist acceptance in the United Nations and a people with no hostile designs on China, is so bizarre as to defy easy explanation. The result is a feeling of uncertainty about future Chinese behavior so grave as to rule out very little. Given such a situation, the Indians are likely to exercise the utmost care in their efforts to avoid offending the Chinese leaders. This leverage is not so great as to reduce India's military preparations, it is strong enough, though, to help make unlikely any Indian decision to alter the tenuous neutral relationship.

Active Levers

The active levers at work are the following:

Perception of vulnerability to exploitation of domestic political dissatisfaction. The Chinese border attack on India reduced Chinese leverage of this type to the vanishing point. A substantial consensus now exists in India around the conclusion that the Chinese must be resisted. A great many Indian communists share this general feeling and have openly sided with the Soviets in the Sino-Soviet dispute. Furthermore, China's hostility to India has been so blatant that the Chinese are believed to be exploiting to the maximum degree their ability to interfere. Given current strategy Chinese leverage strength is slight. Were this strategy perceived to be altering in a direction of China's seeking friendly relations with India, Chinese leverage of this type could gain considerable strength.

Perceived ability to influence actions of a third country. One of the elements of the Sino-Soviet conflict is differing strategic objectives regarding neutral nations. Soviet strategy calls for friendly relations with neutrals and, since India is believed to have influence with the neutrals, India thereby gains some leverage strength. The Chinese disagree with this strategy and are quite willing to offend neutral states. Consequently India's reputed influence with neutrals offers little if any leverage strength.

China, on the other hand, does have influence with the Soviets although that influence has become largely indirect. Because of their desire to retain leadership of world communism, the Soviets can hardly afford to give credibility to the charge that they have lost determination in their pursuit of the world communist goal. The Soviets therefore will probably avoid being placed in a position of too openly favoring the Indians in their struggle with China. Since India needs Soviet support, Indian leaders are unlikely to try to bring the issue to a head. This places the Chinese in a position to say, in effect, that if the Indians adopt a more belligerent attitude toward China the latter will compel the Soviets to choose between them. Such a choice would be expensive for the Soviets and the Indians regardless of the direction of that choice.

Perceived willingness to alter the type of relationship. The Chinese have demonstrated their willingness to move from a neutral to a hostile relationship with India. The Indians on the other hand have not shown a similar willingness. In the leverage system as a whole this grants China an active leverage advantage that reinforces similar advantages emanating from other levers. India's desire to live at peace with China is strong enough that the Indian government is unlikely to take measures that would provoke the Chinese Communists.

Perception of the possibility of recourse to general or limited conventional war. Here again, the Chinese border attack has added greatly to the credibility of China's willingness to alter the relationship to the point of launching a major attack. Since the Chinese demonstrated their superiority, the Indians have much to lose and little to gain from any such attack and therefore can be presumed to wish to avoid armed conflict. This too then constitutes an active leverage advantage for the Chinese. Considering the interaction of this leverage advantage with others in this system, the Chinese appear to have maintained their ability to prevent India from substantially altering their relationship. India's ability to influence the Chinese is weak indeed.

A comparison of these six leverage systems reinforces the conclusion that basic strategic decisions of the world's primary powers is of fundamental importance in determining the momentary real power relationship of two states. In the last case examined China's shift from a strategy of cementing friendly relations with India to one of humiliating India brought great changes in world power configurations. Though it is doubtful the Chinese wished to do so, their tactics increased American ability to influence India. The Soviet Union lost overall strength in its bilateral relations with India. A comparison also suggests an explanation for the diplomatic difficulties of the United States. Quite clearly the major power defending the status quo is placed in a disadvantageous position relative to that of the anti-status quo and even more the strongly anti-status quo major powers.

The limitation of a study of leverage analysis should be clearly understood. The point has been made several times that the construction of a leverage system gives only one aspect of the power picture. Also the point has been made that a determination of goals must be made before beginning an investigation of the leverage system. The entire purpose of the analysis would be subverted were the analyst to conclude that maximizing one's leverage advantage was an end in itself. Beyond this it should be understood that leverage analysis is essentially static analysis. It deals with those means not involving direct action that are available at a given moment for a government to use in seeking to achieve its objectives. Some insight into historical developments and some long-term relational patterns which may have predictive utility, however, may be gained by constructing leverage systems which existed at various critical points in the relations of two states and comparing those systems.

These examples of leverage systems were given to illustrate the possible analytical utility of the approach. Should the potential seem worth exploring the next step would be to make careful case studies involving several examples of each of the relationship types. The relevance of the leverage picture for the central purpose of this study, the construction of a scheme to evaluate the long-term aspects of a government's foreign policy, will be described in the next chapter.

3 | LONG-RANGE STRATEGY

To DOCUMENT the contention that the American diplomatic style is ad hoc is easy; to deplore the perpetuation of this style is satisfying. But before succumbing to the temptations of self-righteousness the analyst should ask two serious questions. First, is a diplomatic style other than an essentially ad hoc one possible in a democratic society? Second, if a theoretical frame for long-range strategic planning can be devised and if the institutional adjustment that is necessary for the planning and execution of long-range strategy can be made, will the consequences tend to subvert the liberal democratic normative base of government? This study is based on the assumption that an affirmative answer can be given to the first question. Indeed the purpose of this chapter is to suggest a frame for evaluating the long-range strategy of a government's foreign policy and this frame may have prescriptive as well as heuristic utility. But the second question is one that social scientists need to ask in many fields. While attempting to construct value-free theory, many modern theorists may be directly or indirectly contributing to the growth of institutions that could devour the very values they believe in but take pains to keep out of their work.

117

The approach to be developed here has obvious prescriptive implications, but what these amount to is little more than a recipe for manipulation for whatever purposes. The dilemma that emerges is a serious one. Man clearly has the scientific potential to improve world standards of living spectacularly. He also has the potential for sudden and massive self-destruction. If the former is to be achieved and the latter not only avoided but securely proscribed, a social science breakthrough comparable to that in the physical sciences is needed. Therefore, increasingly elaborate and, at the same time, increasingly precise methodological instruments are not only useful, they are vital. Yet the almost universal though implicit aim of these methodological designs is ultimately to improve man's ability to manipulate his economic, social, and political environment. Social science methodologists carefully avoid considering the ends of the manipulation. Those scholars whose approaches bear only indirectly on the prescriptive may not even understand the manipulation potential of their work. But the fact is that both those approaches which furnish keys to an understanding of man's behavior and those which bear directly on the means of manipulating that behavior carry implicit value predispositions. Furthermore, an obvious direction of many of these value predispositions is elitist, not to say authoritarian. These comments are specifically apropos of the approach here, and therefore both in this chapter and in the final chapter the problem of reconciling this approach with liberal democratic norms will be considered.

The analytical device to be proposed here for evaluating the long-term aspects of a government's foreign policy is the construction of an ideal type model of a foreign policy that is concerned with the long-term and a comparison of the model with actual foreign policy. The term "ideal type" is used in the Weberian sense and is therefore not meant to imply desirability. An ideal type, long-term focused foreign policy will not exist in reality and thereby avoids being deflected from course by accidents of personality, bureaucratic shortsightedness, and the dynamics of interest group interactions. The model will consider only those aspects of the milieu that are of vital importance for constructing a policy designed to achieve long-term goals. Such an exercise can provide a base for comparison with real policy and should have both analytical and prescriptive value. If both parallels and divergencies between the ideal type and actual policy are noted, analytical insight into foreign policy behavior can be gained and areas in which remedial action is called for may be seen. That those doing the analysis will conclude that the ideal type construction was defective in important aspects is both inevitable and analytically desirable. This, in fact, should be one of the chief means by which the evaluative frame can be refined. This chapter will draw an outline of an ideal type model foreign policy that is concerned with the long-term. The following chapter will use the model as a basis for constructing an ideal type American policy toward Iran, and this in turn will be compared briefly with actual American-Iranian relations.

The general foreign policy aims of a government in any situation are a given for the purposes of this model. There is no intention here of grading or passing judgment on actual aims of any government in a foreign policy situation. The actual general objectives and the ideal type general objectives must be the same if the purpose of the exercise is to provide a base for comparison from which insights could be gained and propositions drawn. Were some other general objectives, more attractive to the analyst, to be substituted the analytical utility of the scheme would be destroyed.

It is at this point, however, that the manipulative sterility of this approach is most oppressive. As the model is developed feasibility will be tested and a strategic-tactical plan for maximum effectiveness suggested. But the general objective is not questioned. If the policy formulation trends are as described in the introduction, such a model as this which is found to have prescriptive utility will only help reinforce the trend toward a bureaucratic monopoly of foreign policy formulation. However, the model may lend itself also to another use and one that could work against turning over determination of objectives to the foreign policy bureaucracy.

There is no grand design or evil conspiracy responsible for the steady decline in influence of even the American attentive public on foreign policy. The reason for this loss of influence is quite simply the growth in variety and complexity of the situations that policy must deal with. Criticisms of many aspects of foreign policy are frequent and vigorous, especially in an election year, but alternate general objectives that may be advanced are usually so divorced from reality that the concerned bureaucracy cannot be blamed for not taking them seriously. Since the bureaucracy is not really challenged, the dangers implicit in a monopoly of policy determination manifest themselves.

Given the complexity of problem situations, competing nongovernmental elites have a central role to play if the liberal democratic process in foreign policy formulation is to be preserved. These competing elites must be drawn from academic and other nongovernmental specialists whose understanding of particular situations is at least the equal of the bureaucrats'. These people alone, through books, articles, and speeches, can serve the function of providing the interested public with a basis for evaluating our foreign policy. Needless to say, this function is being executed very badly and the academic's failure is even more pronounced than the journalist's. The academic community is communicating very little with the public on matters of policy. Instead it aids in the process of bureaucratic monopoly either by almost total emersion in value-free methodological studies, which directly or indirectly have a manipulative potential, or even more directly it serves the bureaucrat as consultant or project contractor.

The potential of the ideal type model in helping meet this challenge lies with the possibility of exploring alternate objectives. To argue for peace, disarmament, accommodation, or for rollback or

Fortress America may have the effect of easing frustrations, but such arguments are rarely if ever accompanied by a blueprint for execution. This model furnishes the outline of such a blueprint. Since by definition the ideal type model is an abstraction from reality, its use for determining real feasibility is limited. Yet anyone advancing an alternate general objective by following the model would be forced in the process of constructing a strategic-tactical plan to consider carefully practical feasibility.

AN IDEAL TYPE MODEL FOR FOREIGN POLICY PLANNING

Determining Objectives

The first stage in the ideal type model must be determining the relevant foreign policy objectives. Such objectives are never self-evident; furthermore a simple isolating of specific objectives for a particular foreign policy problem area is not enough. Foreign policy objectives must be looked upon as together constituting a system of action a comprehension of which calls for an understanding of interaction patterns. Therefore the first step in this scheme calls for isolating the specific foreign policy objectives and relating these to the system. The approach to be utilized here calls for constructing an abstract of the general foreign policy of a government and people on four levels, descending from the broadly general to the fairly specific. This approach for American foreign policy is illustrated on pages 122–23.

There is implicit in this approach a basic assumption regarding the process of foreign policy formulation: at the highest level of generality of foreign policy objectives, and to a large extent at the second level as well, the determination of objectives is so much the consequence of a little-understood total political process as to be beyond the scope of individual planners. These are the levels at which the attitudes of the politically conscious public generally

I. PRESERVE THE PEACE, WELL-BEING, AND SECURITY OF THE AMERICAN PEOPLE.

A. Contain the U.S.S.R., China, Cuba.
1. Deter militarily the primary enemies and their satellites.
   a. Communicate the impression that a nuclear attack would be intolerably expensive.
   b. Communicate the impression that expansion would be too expensive utilizing conventional warfare, guerrilla warfare, encouraged insurgency, or subversion.
   c. Establish and develop military alliances on the communist littoral.
   d. Give unilateral guarantees of support to noncommunist regimes of strategically important states.
2. Encourage the liberalization trends of communist states.
   a. Reinforce the positions of those leaders, frequently consumer-oriented, who perceive coexistence to be possible.
   b. Increase trade selectively as liberalization trend becomes manifest.
3. Encourage tendencies toward autonomy in satellite states.
   a. Grant economic aid selectively and, where autonomy is well established, military aid.
   b. Encourage trade patterns reducing satellite dependence on the U.S.S.R. or China.
4. Work for the economic stability and the economic, military, and political integration of developed noncommunist states.

B. Avoid thermonuclear war.
1. Deter any nuclear power from launching a nuclear attack.
   a. Develop weapons system necessary to make any attack intolerably expensive.
   b. Develop credibility for the use of these weapons.
2. Proscribe certain military behavior.
   a. Set the stage for phased disarmament.
   b. Outlaw certain procedures such as above-ground nuclear testing.
3. Stabilize accidental war areas.
   a. States divided as a result of the Cold War: Germany, Korea, Vietnam, China.
   b. Conflict situations in which the great powers are not directly involved: Arab-Israeli, Kashmir, Cyprus, South Africa.
4. Support and encourage international organizations.
   a. Work to preserve the peacemaking prerogatives of the United Nations.
   b. Support a vigorous role for the Secretary General.
   c. Encourage international cooperation generally through the United Nations, the specialized agencies, and regional organizations.
5. Work for the development of international law.
   a. Observe accepted international law.
   b. Support the International Court of Justice in current practices.

C. Satisfy the economic and other internationally relevant demands of the American people.
1. Provide for the health of the American economy.
   a. Maintain the balance of payments.
   b. Dispose of the agricultural surplus.
   c. Protect against the impact of economic crises abroad.
2. Support American industry and agriculture.
   a. Negotiate tariff reductions for competitive American industries.
   b. Seek agreement on protection for less competitive American industries.
   c. Help American citizens and industries invest and gain contracts abroad.
3. Give diplomatic support and assistence to people for whom there is special concern.
   a. Support the independence and well-being of Israel.
   b. Help improve conditions for the people of Eastern Europe.
   c. Support the independence drive of African peoples.
4. Encourage democracy, support independence, and advance welfare of other peoples.
   a. Establish especially friendly relations with democratic states, aloof but correct relations with authoritarian regimes.
   b. Engage in aid projects and encourage the use of the U.N.

a. Advance credit and monetary support where necessary.
b. Provide diplomatic support for integrationist moves.
c. Encourage the evolution of military pacts into the institutional base for broader alliances.

5. Work for noncommunist stability in developing states.
a. Grant economic and technical assistance necessary to produce stability, short- and long-run.
b. Support economic aid through regional and international agencies.
c. Encourage investment, domestic and foreign.
d. Grant military assistance to enable an embattled noncommunist regime to withstand a communist challenge.
e. Through symbol manipulation present case for development outside communist frame.
f. Through overt and covert diplomacy develop stable regime capable of withstanding the communist challenge.

simply for humanitarian purposes.
5. Ensure that the prestige and dignity of the United States are at all times protected.

will play a significant boundary-drawing role either directly or indirectly. For example, Soviet leaders may pay very little attention to the general foreign policy attitudes of the Soviet public. But if they perceive a significant public demand for an increase in the production of consumer items and a restiveness with the priority system that emphasizes heavy industry geared for producing military equipment, their response may well have vital consequences for the basic Soviet foreign policy stance. Public attitudes, nongovernmental interest group activities, relevant bureaucratic role activities, and leadership attitudes will together set the boundaries for dealing with perceived nondomestic problem areas.

At the first and most general level the questions to be asked include the following: Is the foreign policy essentially "status quo" or "imperialist" in the sense that Morgenthau uses these terms[1]— i.e., are the government and people of a state satisfied with the world configuration of power or do they desire to see an extension of their influence abroad? Are they content with the current world system in which the nation state is the primary terminal political unit? How high a premium is placed on the goal of peace? In the American illustration the proposed answers to these questions are that the American government and people are satisfied with the existing world configuration of power and wish to preserve it, are content with the nation state as the primary terminal political unit, and place a high premium on peace. These answers are implicit in the description of first-level American foreign policy objectives as designed to "preserve the peace, well-being, and security of the American people."

These most basic objectives are momentary although they are unlikely to change rapidly unless under the impact of an internal or external catastrophe. Individual decision makers, even presidents, have a very limited ability to alter these answers and the

1. Hans Morgenthau, *Politics Among Nations,* 3d ed. (New York, 1960), pp. 38–86.

resulting objectives. For example, there are circumstantial grounds for believing that President Kennedy was pushing in a direction that would alter two of these answers. His policy in the Dominican Republic and in Peru, which sought actively to advance liberal democracy in those states, can be explained in terms of advancing American security. But there is a large suspicion that advancing liberal democracy in Latin America was also an end for Kennedy. If so, such a policy would amount subtly to an extension of American influence. Morgenthau refers to this phenomenon as nationalistic universalism.[2] Kennedy in addition was a strong advocate of measures that would integrate the United States in the Atlantic Community. On occasion his calls for North Atlantic cooperation were on a level that could be interpreted as suggesting the eventual creation of a great multinational state.[3]

If it is assumed that Kennedy did indeed have these goals in mind, American foreign policy objectives on the first level for him could be phrased as follows: to preserve the peace, well-being, and security of the American people; to furnish leadership for spreading liberal democracy to Latin America and other developing areas; to work toward the military, economic, and political integration of the North Atlantic area. But even were this the case Kennedy as president would have done no more than gently prod in the direction of the amendments to the original statement. There were no general public attitudes favoring these objectives and no important interest groups, public or governmental, that actively favored them. Kennedy could articulate these objectives without raising too many objections. In each case the suggested policy course coincided with accepted symbols of the American public. But if he had tried to translate them into third- and fourth-level objectives he would soon have learned that he had crossed the implicit boundaries. For example, the culmination of the Kennedy administration's intervention

2. *Ibid.,* pp. 335–46.
3. *The New York Times,* July 5, 1962, pp. 1, 2.

in the Dominican Republic was the election of Juan Bosch to the presidency. Six months later Bosch was overthrown by a military coup. Had Kennedy made the effort to prevent the overthrow of Bosch he would surely have been confronted with intense opposition from members of Congress and from leading elements of the bureaucracy. With regard to North Atlantic integration, Kennedy was sharply limited in the kind of economic concessions he could have persuaded the American polity to make.

If the same basic questions were to be asked of the policy of Great Britain prior to World War II a proposed phraseology of objectives would be: to preserve the peace, well-being, and security of the people of Great Britain and of the Commonwealth. The same question asked of Great Britain's current policy could be given the same answer except with the words "and the Commonwealth" deleted. A decade hence the phraseology might well be: to preserve the peace, well-being, and security of the people of Great Britain and to work for the political, military, and economic integration of Europe. This reflects an assumption here that the British political process is leading the British government from an acceptance of the empire as the primary terminal political unit to the nation state and on toward the creation of a European multinational state.

French foreign policy illustrates what must be the maximum influence of an individual. Prior to 1958 French basic policy objectives could be viewed as the same as British policy is expected to be a decade hence—to preserve the peace, well-being, and security of the French people and to work for the economic, military, and political integration of Europe. But in 1958 this general statement suddenly ceased to be valid. The Algerian crisis affected the French political process in such a way as to result in a virtual abdication to the leadership of De Gaulle. Since De Gaulle had never agreed with the implicit conclusion of Fourth Republic foreign policy that the nation state must be replaced as the terminal unit and was deeply dissatisfied with the influence France exerted on world affairs, he altered French foreign policy fundamentally. Basic policy objectives could now read: to preserve the peace, well-being, and security of the French people and to provide political and military leadership in a restricted European confederation. As such, in Morgenthau's sense, this is an imperialist foreign policy. The 1965 French elections indicated that the days of unquestioning acceptance of De Gaulle's leadership were over. Manifestations of this change in French foreign policy should soon appear in the form of De Gaulle's having serious difficulty in working toward foreign policy objectives on the third and fourth levels.

Soviet foreign policy on this basic level is proposed to read as follows: to preserve the peace, well-being, and security of the Soviet peoples and to furnish leadership for advancing the dialectical process toward world communism. Again in Morgenthau's sense this amounts to an imperialist foreign policy. It is also one that does not look to the nation state as the primary terminal political unit. But at the same time it is descriptive of a policy that is unlikely to be highly aggressive. To the extent that the Soviet Union seeks to expand its influence it does so in the form of actively spreading an ideology, and for many Soviet leaders the influence implications of such a policy are probably not recognized.[4] This is a far cry from the imperialist German objectives under Hitler. There the objective of peace was at a discount and the desire to spread German influence per se was openly proclaimed.

The second level translates the basic objectives into broad, general policy. The term "strategy" is inappropriate for this level of policy because it implies far too much conscious weighing of alternatives by the governmental policy makers. Containment is the term used to describe the policy which followed from a wide-

---

4. This point is well illustrated in Arthur Schlesinger's description of the Kennedy-Khrushchev confrontation in Vienna (Arthur Schlesinger, Jr., *A Thousand Days: John F. Kennedy in the White House* [Cambridge, Mass., 1965], pp. 358–65).

spread American perception that American security interests were threatened by the communist Soviet regime. To think of that policy as the child of the Truman administration and with George Kennan as the theoretical father is to personalize a process that in fact involved much of the American public and bureaucracy. Once the American public after World War II generally perceived a serious threat from the U.S.S.R. the basic alternatives in dealing with that threat were a withdrawal to the western hemisphere (Fortress America), maintaining the status quo (containment), and pushing the Soviet Union back to its prewar area of influence (rollback). Had isolationist attitudes predominated in the United States in the late 1940's the Truman administration could not have inaugurated such policies as NATO, the Marshall Plan, the Truman Doctrine, and Point IV, which fall easily under the umbrella term of containment. And as John Foster Dulles was to learn in 1953 the attitudinal base did not exist for a rollback policy.

Likewise the general policy of avoiding thermonuclear war is a policy translation of the American public and official attitude toward peace as a basic objective. A substantial case could be made, and was made in the days when America's nuclear lead was decisive, for preemptive war as the best means of advancing the long-term peace and security interests of the American people. But, significantly, this argument was not debated in the public arena. This seems to reflect an intuitive recognition of a public attitude that would preclude such a use of force. On the other hand pacifist attitudes or even demands that disarmament proposals be developed and pursued energetically do not appear to characterize a significant section of the public or officialdom. Limited engagements where necessary for containment and a high level of military preparedness spell out the compromise between the objectives of peace and security.

Translating the basic objective of providing for the well-being of the American people into general policy cannot be done so simply.

What constitutes well-being is in fact determined by the interaction of a variety of public attitudes, interest group demands, and role performances of relevant sections of the bureaucracy. Therefore general policy devolving from this objective can probably best be described as measures to "satisfy economic and other internationally relevant demands of the American people."

Really meaningful long-range planning can be done only on the third and even more on the fourth foreign policy levels. At these levels a foreign policy bureaucracy will have far greater freedom of action because of public disinterest or ignorance, the smaller number of concerned interest groups, and a more manageable number of vital variables to deal with. Yet even at the fourth level the relevant variable interactions will be so complex and understanding so limited that planning beyond the immediate future can only be highly tentative at best. As the ideal model being constructed here is developed the implicit conclusion will become apparent that projections into the future must be in outline form only and must be accompanied by built-in devices for testing validity. At this stage in international relations theory probably the most that can be achieved is determining which are the vital variables, how they are to be ordered, and what are some of their patterns of interaction.

The extraordinary problem presented by the interaction of various foreign policy objectives can be illustrated by American policy toward the Arab-Israeli conflict. In the levels of generality-specificity scheme on page 122, the proposition is implicit that in seeking to avoid thermonuclear war the United States seeks to stabilize accidental war situations in which the great powers are not directly involved, and the Arab-Israeli dispute is in this category. However, anyone seeking to construct a long-range plan for achieving this objective would very quickly be made aware of the fact that among the demands of the American people that call for satisfaction is the demand that the independence of Israel and the well-being of the Israeli people be of special concern to the American government. The existence of this demand and of a strong pressure group that articulates the demand amounts to a major limitation on the freedom of action of the concerned foreign policy bureaucracy.

On the other hand a subordinate objective of the general policy of containing the Soviet Union is to work for the noncommunist stability of developing states. Because of their geographical location the Arab states are of particular concern here. The planner for an American policy toward the Arab-Israeli conflict therefore must be equally attentive to the demands of noncommunist stability in the Arab states. This too acts to restrict considerably the planner's freedom of action.

American policy in Vietnam certainly does not provide an illustration of long-term planning, but it does furnish an excellent example of interactions that affect the second level of policy objectives. To begin with, American objectives in Vietnam, as in the Arab-Israeli conflict, were primarily to stabilize an accidental war area. Vietnam, after the Geneva Agreements were concluded, became one of those states divided as a consequence of involvement in the Cold War. The essential problem in such areas is to control the inevitable nationalist demands for unification until the Cold War has altered to a point at which a unified state with a government acceptable to both sides is possible. This presented the American government with the task of helping construct in South Vietnam a noncommunist government capable of maintaining control. By mid-1963, however, it was obvious that the United States, for whatever reasons, was failing in this task. An escalation of the conflict from the guerrilla warfare level seemed probable, and without increased American involvement a unification of the country under a communist regime was also probable. At this point the objective of containing the Soviet Union and China through a policy of conventional warfare deterrence became of equal or even greater importance to the United States than simply stabilizing an accidental war area. American policy makers perceived that a communist success in Vietnam would encourage the Soviets and much more the Chinese to support other "wars of liberation."

The decision made at that time was to increase substantially American commitments of support to the South Vietnamese. This involved taking actions clearly prohibited by the Geneva Agreements. The United States had not signed the Agreements but had expressed general approval and therefore could expect to be roundly denounced by the communists and much of the neutralist world as well. These verbal denunciations of American action, however, were not necessarily predictive of a deterioration of relations. As the Cold War had evolved both sides had come to tolerate energetic action on behalf of one's ally in situations involving divided nations. By late 1964, however, it was finally clear that American forces must be committed directly, not simply as support forces, if a communist victory in South Vietnam was to be prevented. Such a decision was a most serious one and did involve risking a response from China and the Soviet Union that could broaden the conflict. But even direct action of this nature might have remained below the tolerance threshold had the additional forces confined their activities to South Vietnam.

This latter point, however, must remain conjecture, for the decision was made to combine the direct use of force in South Vietnam with bombing of North Vietnam. For at least two elements of the concerned bureaucracy the decision to bomb North Vietnam was a necessary one. The seeming illogic of granting the communists a sanctuary in North Vietnam and of doing nothing substantial to halt the flow of arms from there was oppressive to those members of the military bureaucracy responsible for the lives of American servicemen. This response was only to be expected, but it might not have carried the day if there had not been a less easily anticipated and complementary response from another source.

There has appeared in the last decade a group of semiacademic, semibureaucratic theorists concerned with the area of strategic planning. Because their advice is so frequently solicited and their writings so widely read inside the bureaucracy, one can presume their influence is substantial. To the extent that they concern themselves with diplomacy, the claim of Thomas Schelling[5] seems to prevail that diplomacy can be viewed as a bargaining process which is reducible to some general bargaining rules. Left out are the situational determinants of bargaining, which in this study are incorporated in the leverage system, in particular those less manipulatable levers referred to as passive. The tendency exists in this group therefore to view such actions as the bombing of North Vietnam in bargaining terms, the threat of graduated reprisals being an obvious example. The situational impact of developing credibility for such a threat—and the bombings can be viewed in these terms—was largely ignored.

There is much circumstantial evidence of conflict between those members of the bureaucracy who viewed the bombings primarily as a means to reduce the capability of the enemy and those who viewed them as aspects of bargaining. The former group, for example, had the greatest difficulty comprehending the decision to spare the most important capability targets in North Vietnam, Hanoi and Haiphong.[6] Viewed as a bargaining device, however, such restraint was only sensible. The threat to expand targets had real credibility, especially since the North Vietnamese must have been aware of the school of thought in the American bureaucracy that favored further escalation.

The point to be made here, however, is that neither group ap-

5. Thomas Schelling, *Arms and Influence* (New Haven, Conn., 1966), pp. 1–34.

6. See for example a report by James Reston in *The New York Times,* March 23, 1966, p. 46, and the remarks of Senator Symington, also in the *Times,* March 30, 1966, p. 37.

peared to be aware of the general policy objective implications of those bombings. In fact these implications are manifest in most of the third- and fourth-level objectives as well. Senator Fulbright in a series of lectures spoke of the dynamics of the arrogance of power and wondered if even the basic status quo foreign policy stance of this country were not threatened.[7] His argument was badly misunderstood at the time. He was referring to a process of objective alteration that is not only not directed by power-hungry men but is not even understood by the relevant decision makers. This is much the same point as is being made here.

That bombings of North Vietnam should have so much greater an impact than bombings of communist-dominated areas of South Vietnam is due to the greater difficulty of explaining the former action simply in containment terms. Similar difficulty was encountered with the decision to cross the 38th parallel in Korea after the initial North Korean thrust into South Korea was defeated. But the sudden and open invasion of South Korea was a far more clear-cut challenge to the status quo the United States was defending than was the infiltrating of arms and men into South Vietnam to aid guerrillas who were overwhelmingly men of South Vietnamese origin. More comparable was the demand from Douglas MacArthur for bombing north of the Yalu. And the argument against MacArthur's suggestion was in essence the same as that regarding Vietnam: it could result in a basic alteration of the established mode of behavior of the Cold War, in which direct confrontation was to be of a limited nature.

Most directly and adversely affected of the third-level objectives was the encouragement of the liberalization trends of communist states. A relevant fourth-level objective was to strengthen the position of those communist officials who believe coexistence is possible.

7. *Ibid.,* May 1, 1966, Sec. 4, p. 10. See also William J. Fulbright, *The Arrogance of Power* (New York, 1967).

The very real danger was that the American actions would be interpreted as going well beyond the needs of containment and in fact constituting the beginnings of more or less planned aggression. Should such a perceptual alteration occur, the position of those who had not really accepted coexistence as a possibility would surely be strengthened at the expense of the advocates of coexistence. The interaction of any such changes in communist leadership with American policy would likely result in an intensification of the conflict and therefore in a reinforcement of the argument of the American politicians and bureaucrats who have been ready to accept battle with North Vietnam on the soil of North Vietnam and who have seen merit in preemptive nuclear warfare with China before the latter could develop a long range delivery system and a nuclear stock pile. If these changes were to occur, the second-level objectives of "containment" and "avoiding thermonuclear war" would be threatened with replacement by "rollback" and "preemptive nuclear warfare." This is an illustration of what is meant by a basic alteration in the established mode of behavior of the Cold War.

Another third-level objective which was adversely affected was that of working for the economic, military, and political integration of developed noncommunist states. Of course this objective had already been adversely affected by the decline in the intensity of the perceived threat from the Soviet Union. Without such a decline there is little likelihood that the divisive policy of De Gaulle could have made much progress. But this perceptual change, added to Europe's increasing fear of involvement in an unnecessary war with China resulting from the American alliance, weakened the integration trend.

Of course, only the exceptional foreign policy problem will have this kind of systemic involvement, but each one must be viewed in the perspective of the system of aims.

Situational Analysis

Once the general objective for the particular foreign policy problem has been determined and related to the foreign policy aims system, the second step in the ideal type model is to construct an operationally useful estimate of the situation. This task is primarily one of creating analytical order. The analytical ordering device to be utilized here will be the relevant trend system.

A foreign policy that is designed to look to and influence future developments will be implicitly concerned with trend manipulation. Sometimes, as in the Alliance for Progress, some of the trends that are of concern will be pointed to specifically. More frequently, however, this will be done rather inadvertently as a spill-over from an attempt to achieve a more concretely perceived goal, as in containment of the great communist states. The assumption here is that much can be learned about a long-term focused foreign policy by comparing it with an ideal type construct in which the relevant trends have been made explicit. In the ideal type model long-term foreign policy will amount to the optimum manipulation of relevant long-term trends. Optimum in this case means, with a given capability, having the greatest possible effect in altering long-term trends in a direction consistent with policy objectives. Trend alteration will involve reinforcing some trends, redirecting others, and reversing some.

The problems presented by trend analysis are massive indeed. Not only must the basic trends be identified and subjected to the most searching qualitative and quantitative analysis, but a prior decision must be made as to what constitutes the basic relevant trends. In any situation the number of trends that could be considered approaches the infinite. Furthermore, opinions as to which trends are relevant would vary almost to the same degree. Any model scheme must therefore present a list of general categories or typology of trends that in any situation should be the relevant ones. Such a list will provide some order for trend analysis and also will likely point to vital trends whose importance has gone unnoticed.

A list of relevant trend categories will be advanced here without developing the argument that these are indeed the most relevant categories. In another study a description of the genesis of this list and a development of a case for the utility of those categories will be made.[8] Here the list is merely advanced as a useful one for meeting the needs of the scheme. In the following chapter the utility of this list will be given a test in the case of American policy toward Iran. The categories are as follows:

1) Trends in power potential rating
2) Trends producing or discouraging mass participation
3) Trends in elite relationships, public, political, and bureaucratic
4) Trends in relevant sections of elite and mass value systems
5) Trends in relevant sections of elite and mass perceptions
6) Trends in relevant sections of elite and mass attitudes

The first task in the ideal type model, therefore, is to make a situational analysis with the objective of identifying and describing the relevant long-term trends. The systemic relatedness of these trends becomes apparent by merely listing them. Interactions will be made explicit however in the strategic and tactical steps of the ideal type model. In the following chapter the situational analysis will concern a bilateral relationship, but the model should be adaptable to a multilateral relationship as well.

Determining Capability

In Chapter Two the proposition was advanced that the momentary power of a state depends on the power potential factors of that

8. In a case study of the British in Egypt.

state and on the strategic interactions of the government of that state with others, particularly states in the first power category. As was pointed out then, there is no simple recipe for rating a state in power potential terms because so many of the judgments called for must be subjective, for example, national character. In this chapter each state will be classified in one of five power categories based on an arbitrary assessment of the sum of the power factors. In the preceding section "trends in power potential ratings" was listed as one of the vital trend categories and therefore this aspect of the power picture has already been presented.

The operationally more significant aspect of the power picture is that relating to strategic interaction. In Chapter Two the leverage system construct was advanced as a means for translating these strategic interactions into influence terms. Capability determination in the ideal type model, therefore, will consist of constructing the operative leverage system existing between or among the states concerned in a problem.

Objectives in Terms of Trend Manipulation

The next two steps in the ideal type model are designed to make the general objective operational. The first step calls for translating the general objective into desired trend alteration. Each of the trends therefore should be examined from the point of view of their utility or disutility in reaching the stated objectives. Then the objective can be expressed in terms of ignoring, reinforcing, redirecting, or reversing relevant trends.

Objectives and Capability

At this point the general objective translated in terms of long-term trend alteration is in effect what the objective would be if there were few limits to capability. A moment's reflection, however, should reveal that the actor government lacks the capability of reversing or seriously redirecting many vital trends. Therefore, the fifth task in the ideal type model is to redefine the general objective in terms of an altering of long-term trends to a degree consonant with the real power of the actor government. The power of the actor government will have been spelled out in the form of the operative leverage system. What this task amounts to therefore is an exploring of the leverage potential for influencing the target government in order to bring about desired trend alteration.

Constructing a Strategy

After completing the above task, the analyst will be ready to construct a basic strategy, the sixth step in setting up the ideal type model. As will be readily apparent from the Iranian example in the following chapter, constructing a strategy involves a great deal more than merely spelling out the implications of the above section in which the desired trend alteration was correlated with capability. Most of the relevant trends that will be identified and described in the situational analysis will not be classifiable as either advantageous or deleterious with regard to the achievement of the objectives, and therefore in spelling out the objective in terms of trend alteration they will be ignored. Once a strategic decision has been made, however, many of these previously ignored trends will suddenly be of significance in any tactical plan for the execution of this decision. Trend interaction is such that any strategic program will necessarily be concerned with expected effects on most of the relevant trends.

The construction of a strategy, therefore, involves first a decision as to how the desired trend alteration can be achieved without in the process so influencing other trends as to create a new trend system that in important respects runs counter to the general objective. Having made this decision, the strategist must then spell out a strategic program in terms of trend alteration (now involving many trends that were previously ignored) for which his government has the capability.

Tactical Planning: The Diplomatic Probe

The final task in constructing the ideal type model is to devise a tactical plan for the achievement of the strategic program. Up to this point it may seem to have been an implicit assumption that the situational analysis would provide a reasonably clear picture of the relevant trends, the behavior of the trend system, the important levers, and the behavior of the leverage system. In fact, of course, the situational analysis will consist of a number of tentative judgments, hypotheses, and simple conjectures. Tactical planning from a base such as this would require much courage even for the analyst working with the ideal type model. There can be little wonder then that the foreign policy bureaucrat prefers making decisions day by day.

An essential part of this scheme is to incorporate in the tactical planning stage of the model a means for testing and exploring some of the judgments, hypotheses, and conjectures of the situational analysis. The device suggested for this purpose is once again an ancient one, the diplomatic probe. Man has been conducting diplomatic probes for as long as he has been organized in political groups with competing interests. In modern times, diplomatic probing techniques have reflected the increasing complexity of intergovernmental relations and some probes of great imagination and subtlety have been conducted. But neither scholars nor practitioners have made any real effort to develop the analytical and prescriptive potential of the diplomatic probe.

For the analyst, the diplomatic probe comes close to providing the social scientist's dream of a controlled laboratory situation. Although there will always be a wide variety of complicating variables in any situation to be probed, several different probes involving different variable combinations can sometimes be devised which, when compared, may offer some important insights. Through the use of the probes major hypotheses regarding trends, levers, and their system interactions can be tested. If expected behavior occurs, the analyst can have greater confidence in his situational analysis. Should results differ from expectations, a searching revision of the hypotheses, followed by further probing, will be in order. For the practitioner, the utility of the probe lies in testing the validity of the suppositions behind a strategic program.

The first stage of the task of tactical planning in the ideal type model is therefore to make a list of those hypotheses regarding trends, levers, and their system interactions that need to be tested. The second stage will be to explore the possibility of constructing one or several probes that will not commit the actor government to a policy line but will test the important hypotheses.

Probing operations can be placed in two general categories: probes that can be conducted prior to inauguration of a tactical scheme without committing the actor government to any specific policy line, and probes that are incorporated in the tactical scheme. The policy-independent, or "one-shot," probes are difficult to devise and more tentative in results, but they have the advantage of permitting a refinement of strategic programming and tactical planning without the risks involved in policy execution. For anyone using the ideal type model, however, the scheme can be carried no further than the compilation of hypotheses to be tested and a construction of one-shot probes for testing the hypotheses.

Many of the most successful probes are conducted inadvertently, and for the scholar who is denied access to the practitioners' plans all probes will have the appearance of inadvertence. This need not affect the analytical utility of these probes, however. The skilled analyst can easily construct or reconstruct the probe and discover whatever insights are thereby revealed. Of course this can be true only of those probes that are of such a scope as to attract public attention. But these will be the more important ones.

Thus far the analytical and prescriptive potential of the one-shot probe has barely been explored. Any skilled diplomat will in his normal diplomatic contacts attempt to probe deeply into the attitudes, motivations, and objectives of target personalities but beyond this little is done. There is reason to believe, however, that Soviet diplomacy does carry one-shot probing somewhat further. In any case, advertently or inadvertently, the Soviets did some important probing in the latter part of 1961, which will be outlined for purposes of illustrating the one-shot probe.

It is assumed here that a major aspect of Soviet strategy in 1961 was to devise some tactical plans for at least weakening the trend toward western European integration. In any such planning, Soviet leaders could hardly overlook the value of playing on historical fears of Germany in western Europe. Any strong manifestation of a revitalized German nationalism should be of considerable value in keeping strong the fear of renewed German aggression. Considering the close relations and cooperation of Germans with other Europeans, however, the hypothesis could be advanced that there was a long-term trend toward a rapid decline of the fear of Germany. Also, indications such as the declining use of nationalism in West German elections could lead to a second major hypothesis, that there was a long-term trend away from national values and nationalistic attitudes in West Germany. Should verification for these trends be gained, a reappraisal of Soviet ability to weaken significantly the European integration trend might be in order.

In late October, 1961, the Soviet Union invoked the section of the Finno-Soviet treaty that gives either party the right to call for joint defense consultations.[9] The timing of the note added to the sense of urgency. President Kekkonen of Finland was in Hawaii and was compelled to rush back to Finland. Observers at the time viewed the note as possibly the kickoff for a major Soviet diplomatic offensive against Scandinavia.[10] But the text of the note was overwhelmingly concerned with the danger to the Scandinavian nations

9. *The New York Times,* October 31, 1961, pp. 1, 12.
10. *Ibid.,* November 1, 1961, p. 1.

implicit in the alleged revival of German militarism. No anti-Scandinavian offensive materialized, and the conclusion is at least plausible that this was a fairly elaborate one-shot probe of the hypotheses concerning the fear of Germany and German nationalism.

Whether by design or not, the issuance of the note preceded by only a few days a projected visit to Oslo by, of all people, German Defense Minister Strauss. No German leader better fits the stereotype of the new breed of German militarists. The coincidence of the note and the projected visit did provide the basis for an excellent probing operation, and the results were hardly reassuring. German reaction could only stand as evidence of the decline of German nationalism. There was no indignant public outcry insisting that Strauss follow through with his planned visit, as would be expected from volatile nationalists. Instead an embarrassed German government decided that more would be lost by canceling the visit and Strauss went to Oslo.[11] This decision was met by a loud outcry from President Kekkonen, who called a visit at this time a blunder.[12] But such a reaction need indicate nothing more than an overly anxious response to a threat to friendly Finno-Soviet relations. In Oslo, however, there was some good evidence that the fear and dislike of Germany remained strong. Anti-Strauss demonstrations plagued the entire visit and served to embarrass both the German and Norwegian governments. No lasting damage was done German-Norwegian relations, however, which indicates that fear of Germany in Norway was not great enough to compel the Norwegian government to alter its policy. Confirmatory evidence was thereby given for the conclusion that fear of Germany was declining in Scandinavia.

Two weeks later Ambassador Hans Kroll, then representing Bonn in Moscow, presented the Soviets with a probe of the two hypotheses. In conversations with Premier Khrushchev he initiated a discussion of a program for rapprochement that would begin with

11. *Ibid.,* November 18, 1961, p. 7.
12. *Ibid.,* November 20, 1961, p. 6.

specified settlements. Somehow the substance of these conversations was leaked to the world press.[13] Ambassador Kroll's erratic behavior was well understood in many capitals. Nevertheless in the days that followed there was a great deal of nervous speculation in western Europe of a possible new Rapallo.[14] But this was the extent of the severity of reaction, and as such it followed closely the pattern of the Scandinavian probe. There was clear evidence of continued fear and distrust of Germany but the mildness of German reaction, or lack of it, to Kroll's proposal was even more telling. If a revival of German nationalism were likely, the opportunities that were presented to carry out an independent policy and to play East against West would seem to make the Kroll conversations exciting news. And there was enough of a favorable response to make it difficult for Chancellor Adenauer to remove a troublesome diplomat. But the response hardly pointed to strong but latent German nationalism.

Shortly later the Soviets renewed their verbal assaults on General Adolf Heusinger, a leading West German military personality attached to NATO, for his allegedly heavy war crimes record. Again reaction fell into the familiar pattern. Some western European papers did fret about General Heusinger, but the reaction was not strong enough to lead to any serious demand for Heusinger's removal.[15] Within Germany there was not the indignant reaction that could be expected from a highly nationalistic population.

Were these in fact carefully designed and coordinated diplomatic probes on the Soviet part, they succeeded in painting a picture of an at least temporarily declining fear of Germany and an at least temporarily quiescent nationalism in Germany. These were not the

13. According to *Newsweek*, November 20, 1961, p. 42, the report was "leaked from Moscow to the western press before western diplomats were notified officially."

14. *The New York Times,* November 18, 1961, p. 1.

15. See *The New York Times,* December 13, 1961, p. 1; December 17, 1961, Sec. 4, p. 5; December 19, 1961, p. 3.

results that could make promising the use of fear of Germany and a revival of German nationalism in tactical plans for countering the European integration trend.

Diplomatic probes, as these examples indicate, can take a wide variety of forms. Some of the more common types in American diplomacy will be described below. But in altering the diplomatic style to more closely adhere to the modern era, a much more inclusive typology will be necessary.

1) *Probes involving conversations with target personalities.* Direct probing through diplomatic conversations, as indicated above, is the one variety of diplomatic probe that is standard operating procedure. All diplomats use eliciting and provocation techniques to probe the attitudes and policies of target personalities. The importance of this technique can hardly be overestimated. In order to be successful, the diplomat must have a thorough comprehension of the general situation and the immediate problem, an understanding of the leading target personalities, an acute social sensitivity, and a sense of timing and aplomb. The most common deficiency in the American diplomat is in the area of an understanding of the general situation and, in particular, of target actor perceptions. He is likely to be well briefed on the immediate problem, however.

Indirect probing through diplomatic conversations is another form of this type of probe. In any diplomatic community certain ambassadors and lesser diplomats will be strikingly successful in developing rapport with leading personalities of the host country. This opens the door to the possibility of using a diplomat of a third country for a probing operation. Where relations are close with the particular third country, the probe can possibly be arranged directly. Where this is not the case, the same type of probing operation must be conducted against the third country diplomat as against the original target personality. But access should be easier.

Indirect probing can utilize nonofficial Americans in a target country who are close to various target personalities. Conducting a probe through such individuals presents many difficulties. Only rarely will they have the comprehension and professional skills of the diplomat. Furthermore the diplomat runs a severe risk of being unable to control a probe being carried out by the nonofficial American. Still the type of relationship a nonofficial American will have with a target personality is likely to be different from that which is possible for the diplomat and may well be on a more candid plane. The potential reward, therefore, may be worth the time and care necessary in planning a probe through a nonofficial American regardless of the risk involved.

Indirect probing utilizing nonofficial persons of a third country involves both greater risk and greater potential reward than working through a nonofficial American. The reward can be greater because the target personality is likely to feel less constraint in his conversations relating to matters of interest to the United States when he is speaking with citizens of a third country than when speaking with an American. The risk is greater because the problem of control is greater. But the very increased difficulty may be an asset. The American diplomat will lack the temptation to take such an individual into his confidence and will plan from the beginning a plausible and seemingly innocent reason for persuading the third country person to do his probing.

Indirect probing utilizing nonofficial indigenous persons presents problems and potentials similar to those discussed above. Where the relationship with the indigenous person is a quasi-agent one, the control problem will not be as serious. This type of relationship is more common than is realized—even by many American diplomats. Particularly in those states with a history of indirect formal or nonformal colonial relationship with a western power, some citizens of the host state will in fact seek to gain the reputation of being "close" to the Americans. When this reputation has been gained, the individual involved will not be likely to have a candid relationship with target personalities. For probes of probable reactions to possible American policy lines, however, they can be invaluable.

2) *Probes involving planted but nonattributable rumors.* A well-planned rumor campaign can be one of the most effective types of probing operations. It can be utilized to test unknowns and tentative hypotheses regarding the attitudes and motivations of leading personalities and the attitudes of political groups and the various publics. However, the nonattributable rumor presents many serious mechanical problems. For the hypotheses to be tested well, those through whom the rumor is to be spread must be carefully selected from the points of view of access and credibility. Planting the nonattributable rumor with such individuals requires the utmost ingenuity.

3) *Probes involving nonattributable written material.* One variety of this type of probe is black written material—that which is attributed to a source other than the originator and without the knowledge or consent of the attributed source. An example of this would be the production by Americans of a pamphlet that purports to be a communist publication of a target country. The pamphlet must be substantively and stylistically credible and the distribution pattern and channels must be authentic. This is often technically feasible. Since communist parties are frequently at least semicovert, the distribution channels for their printed material will not be known to most recipients and a parallel channel set up by Americans for distribution of the black material would seem to those recipients to be authentic. Black written material is not an uncommonly used weapon in the Cold War, but its use is largely confined to psychological warfare. The potential for probing operations may be a rich one but, so far as is known, it has been little explored.

The decision to use black material should not be made lightly despite its feasibility. Short-run nonattributability may be achieved but ultimate disclosure could produce a boomerang effect, which would more than counterbalance the brief gain. The image a foreign office is seeking to project might well be affected adversely. It is important throughout a consideration of a typology of probes to keep in mind the fact that probes are a means toward an end and must never be permitted to consume or subvert those ends. For those assigned the task of developing them, the creation of ingenious probes could easily become an end.

Planting articles in newspapers is a common practice in many areas of the world. In fact, outside the Anglo-Saxon and totalitarian states space in many newspapers and sometimes in a majority of papers is for sale. The probing potential here is obviously a rich one. The hypotheses to be probed will of course determine the type of journal to be utilized. If a wide variety of journals in a target state is available for utilization, a sophisticated probing operation could produce a very revealing patterned reaction.

For those newspapers and journals which are closed to outright purchase of space, and this includes all the important American papers, the inspired article can serve as a very important probing device. This is particularly true regarding American papers that are read in states in which the government traditionally has an active influence in newspaper policy. In these states papers such as the *New York Times* will be regarded as at least giving semi-official expression to American governmental views. Even where the role of the American press is better understood, the influence of leading American journals with the informed public and the foreign policy bureaucracy is a matter of concern. Therefore the tone and specific comments of the American journal will be noted and reacted to.

Any suggestion that the American government should inspire articles in the American press no doubt will and certainly should give rise to some fundamental objections. If such a practice were engaged in at all extensively the charge of a managed press could legitimately be raised. Yet absolute proscription of this practice is probably an impossibility. The State Department, American embassies, and the United States Information Agency will always be a primary source of information for journalists and the information they furnish will always be carefully selected. The American journalist stationed abroad who relies excessively on official American sources for his background information may easily become unwittingly but in effect an American propagandist. In the long run the only real defense against government management of the news is excellent reporting. And probably the most that can be hoped for in placing controls over the bureaucracy is that the information given reporters is neither misleading nor inaccurate. To institutionalize even this type of control would be extraordinarily difficult.

A hypothetical example of an inspired article that could serve as a probe and need not constitute a threat to the freedom of the press is as follows: The United States government is considering placing strong pressure on a Latin American government to reduce official corrupton, which is threatening the very stability of the regime. Before doing so, however, the government wishes to probe public and official sensitivity to American intervention on this subject. Therefore a responsible American journalist is given several leads to run down for a story on official corruption. Officials and public leaders of the Latin American country are likely to suspect that the resulting article had been inspired, and their reaction could forecast the limits of tolerance for official American intercession in the matter. Were the information given the reporter misleading or erroneous the implications for a free press would be serious indeed. But as long as the story is a legitimate one and the reporter is alert, the danger should be slight. In this case the government action should be directly comparable to a newsworthy tip from a private source. Far more serious and, one suspects, far more common is the practice of interceding with editors to play down news stories that could have an embarrassing effect on official policy.

It is worth noting that if the reporter in the above hypothetical example had come across the same evidence on his own the probe would have been no less effective. In fact, were the American press abroad more alert to important stories the necessity for suggesting any would quickly vanish.

4) *Probes involving official leaks, off-the-record remarks, and studied slips.* The three modes of probing considered in this section have the same general characteristics. They can be utilized for one-shot probing, but official interest is likely to be recognized and a target government may therefore be forewarned of a possible policy line or of a particular interest. Those doing the probing, however, need not be committed to a course of action and, if the results are not as expected, strategic and tactical adjustments can be made.

An official leak is the passing of information by a government official, acting in his official capacity, to an individual with the understanding that this information will be made public but the identity of the official will remain confidential. This device can be used to test either, or both, official or public reactions to an official view or projected course of action. The leak can be easily tailored for a particular target and for a desired degree of credibility.

Off-the-record remarks and background briefings are more secure but less pointed than the official leak. A briefing officer or public official making off-the-record remarks must understand that what he is saying, if it is of any consequence, is likely to appear in the writings of the attending journalists. A variant of the hypothetical case given in the inspired article category could be an example. An American official either in off-the-record remarks or in a background briefing might mention the growing dissatisfaction in the target Latin American state resulting from widespread corruption. Those Washington correspondents who know very little about the target country would probably refer in any relevant article to corruption and resulting dissatisfaction in that country. A discerning officer in the target country embassy might well note this pattern and surmise official involvement, and this could lead to an official reaction. Politicians, both government and opposition, of the target country might well also note the American press pattern and react to it. The United States government would then be in a position to observe the response to this line, and no major disavowal problem would be involved should the reaction indicate that American pressure here would not be tolerated. In a dictatorship a journalistic pattern of response is almost certainly the result of official intervention and therefore can hardly be used as a one-shot probing device. But in a democracy a patterned response could be due to a variety of stimuli and doubt concerning governmental involvement would persist.

Studied slips and conscious ambiguity offer a considerable amount of flexibility in probing. The requirements for both are that some form of reaction from the target develop and that the official involved be able afterward to explain away with credibility the slip or the implications of an ambiguous remark. Depending on the variety of reaction provoked and the objectives sought by the probe, the clarifying statement can confirm, absolutely deny, or reinterpret the meaning perceived by the target. Since slips and ambiguities are omnipresent, the target is likely to grant some credibility to the clarifying remarks although the suspicion will probably remain that there was a conscious purpose involved.

5) *Probes involving statements of persons not directly involved in foreign policy formulation.* Democratic governments are frequently embarrassed by statements with foreign policy implications made by certain irrepressible officials who are not directly concerned with foreign policy. Almost universally overlooked is the potential in this situation for probing operations. Here again the success of the probe depends on impressing the target sufficiently to provoke a reaction but not to the extent of destroying the credibility of a denial. Such a reaction is likely to occur if the suspicion is generated that the talkative official was speaking of a policy proposal under consideration or was reflecting the view of a significant minority faction in the policy community.

This type of probe is not limited to deliberately irresponsible statements. An official only slightly concerned with foreign policy may make a statement that falls within his general purview but has significant foreign policy implications of which he could claim to be unaware. Such matters as reactions to possible changes in United States tariff policy could be explored in this manner.

Statements by leading nonofficial politicians provide a flexibility in probing far greater in the United States, where there is a decentralized party structure, than for example in Great Britain with its centralized and disciplined party system. For probes directed at states that have a comprehension of the American political process, very strong statements can be made by politicians who do not hold federal office, even those of the same party as the president, without seriously disturbing the plausibility of the administration's lack of responsibility for the remarks. The strength of the probe will vary with the stature of the speaker and with his membership in the administration or opposition party. Furthermore, the probe is likely to stimulate a reaction if the target respects the political potential of the speaker regardless of whether official involvement is suspected. There is potential here for sophisticated and carefully phased probing.

Statements by federal legislators afford a type of probing well suited to the United States because of the separation of powers doctrine. Due to the fiercely asserted independence of the Senate and House of Represesntatives considerable credibility will be granted to official denial of responsibility for congressional statements. Furthermore, where the independent influence of Congress in foreign policy is understood, statements by senators and representatives are likely to produce a reaction in the target government regardless of a suspicion of collusion with the Department of State.

A good deal of flexibility in the probing operation is possible here. If the matter to be probed were judged as highly sensitive and possibly capable of producing a vigorous reaction, the choice of a little-known opposition representative would be advisable. For a more pointed probe, a member of the Senate Foreign Relations Committee or House Foreign Affairs Committee could be used. Since these gentlemen can speak knowingly of even obscure problems in important states and of important problems in obscure states, their statements can have a greater range and still not reduce the credibility of an official denial of responsibility. A statement by the chairman of the Senate Foreign Relations Committee, especially if he is of the same party as the president, can be a very sharply pointed probe.

6) *Probes involving official statements or actions directly concerned with foreign policy.* Any foreign policy statement and any foreign policy action will be, whether construed to be such or not, a diplomatic probe. Diplomats will have anticipated a certain reaction to their statements and actions, and the reaction will then be evaluated in the light of these expectations. These expectations and evaluations, however, will generally not be in the form of some carefully drawn up hypotheses and a testing of these hypotheses. Rather both expectations and evaluations are likely to be more felt than consciously elaborated. In the hands of a skilled and knowledgeable diplomat, this probing operation can result in the acquisition of general insight and understanding. But the insight and understanding gained will be only a fraction of that which could be achieved by an approach that combines the diplomat's skill and a systematic and explicit analysis of the unknown and tentative hypotheses that need to be tested.

One-shot probing is possible even using the direct statement-action device. Since any statement and set of actions will have implications for foreign policy matters other than those under direct concern, these statements and actions can be designed as one-shot probes of matters of tangential concern. Of the Soviet probes described earlier, the Finnish note and the attack on General Heusinger could be viewed as one-shot probes of this variety. Both statements were part of a general policy line of disrupting

NATO but the probing of the extent of fear of Germany and of German nationalism was a by-product. A great deal of this type of probing, including possibly the two examples just mentioned, will be an unplanned by-product of existing policy and the academicians and practitioners need only have the wit to recognize it. But in other cases the probe itself may be the primary purpose of the action.

Tactical Planning: Contingent Phasing

The third and final stage of tactical planning is to construct a plan of action for achieving the agreed-upon strategic objectives. Even with optimum success, the second stage of tactical planning, involving one-shot probes, will do no more than strengthen working hypotheses. Consequently the ultimate tactical plan must incorporate a number of probes for further testing hypotheses and unknowns. Also the tactical plan must include planning for contingent developments. Should a central hypothesis prove to be invalid or only partially valid, a plan of action should be available for altering the general tactical scheme. An essential part of the third stage of tactical planning, therefore, is to incorporate plans of action that could be followed if any of a number of plausible contingencies should materialize.

In order to meet these requirements, the ideal type model calls for a contingent phasing outline. The first phase will be concerned with the tactical scheme for the immediate future. Tactical planning in this phase should be very detailed. It will be based on an assumption of validity for a number of important hypotheses; however, included in this planning should be a number of probes designed to test the validity of these hypotheses.

The second phase will include an optimum and a number of contingent tactical schemes. The optimum tactical scheme is that which would be put into effect if the operating hypotheses held up under probing and if the expected trend developments materialized.

Contingent tactical schemes call for an assessment of the most likely alternate probe results and trend developments. Planning in this phase would necessarily be far less detailed since many specific details must wait until the results of the probes are known.

The third phase will be a continuation of the above scheme. There will be an optimal tactical scheme, a number of secondary optimal schemes developing from the various contingent plans in phase two, and further contingent planning from each of the tactical schemes in phase two. Planning in this phase would be even less detailed. Beyond phase three very tentative tactical plans could be outlined for the optimal tactical scheme and some of the more plausible contingency schemes, but to do any detailed planning beyond this phase or to try to take into consideration a great many possible variations would reduce flexibility.

The ideal type model, of course, can go no further than to prepare an ideal type first tactical scheme and to outline second- and third-phase optimal and contingent plans. The assumption here is that the essence of meaningful long-term planning lies in the identification and assessment of vital long-term trends rather than in projections of developments in the far distant future. Trend interaction within any situation is so complex that at this stage of understanding planning very far beyond the immediate future should be in general terms, tentative, and flexible. This static limitation, however, need not prevent the use of the model as a basis for evaluating a foreign policy over a period of time. In order to add a dynamic quality to an essentially static evaluative scheme, the analyst should select a number of key dates in the history of the foreign policy to be evaluated and to construct an ideal type policy for each of these dates. A comparison of the several evaluations should furnish some important insights and lead to explanatory propositions. Reconstructing probes on the basis of historical developments could be a very helpful analytical device but one that is independent of this scheme.

4 THE UNITED STATES AND IRAN

THE CASE of American policy toward Iran has been selected to illustrate the ideal type policy simply because of this writer's area specialty. In one respect the choice is not an altogether happy one. This is an example of a "dependent" relationship, the type in which tolerance for interference is broadest. The ideal type policy outlined below therefore incorporates interference in a broader degree than would be true of any other type of relationship. No case would be typical, however, and the general lines of the ideal type American–Iranian relations will resemble those of any other bilateral relationship.

Since an explanation of this approach calls for a detailed illustration of an ideal type policy, the case study that follows is rather lengthy. In spite of its length, however, the situational analysis concerning Iran is asserted rather than developed. To produce supporting evidence for these assertions would call for an expansion of this chapter into book length and far beyond marginal utility for the purposes here. Furthermore, even if supporting evidence were presented, the assertions would be no more than tentative judgments because conclusive supporting evidence cannot be obtained. This would call for the acquisition of survey research data

155

on subject matter that cannot honestly be explored in a dictatorship. Those readers who wish to see supporting historical evidence for these assertions are referred to my *Nationalism in Iran* (Pittsburgh, Pa., 1964). Other readers should think of the case as hypothetical.

AN IDEAL TYPE MODEL FOR IRAN

Determining Objectives

The aspect of the American foreign policy aims system that is relevant here is the third- and fourth-level objective of working through overt and covert diplomacy to encourage the establishment of a regime in a developing state, Iran, that would be capable of withstanding the communist challenge. As listed in the American foreign policy aims system on page 122, the objectives can be stated as follows: In order to preserve the peace and provide for the security of the American people (level 1) the Soviet Union must be prevented from expanding its influence into the Middle East (level 2). This calls for encouraging stable, non-communist regimes in the developing states of the Middle East, of which Iran is one of the most vital (level 3); and in order to encourage the creation of a regime in Iran capable of resisting an expansion of Soviet influence the United States must develop an effective program for Iran involving both overt and covert diplomacy (level 4).

That the objective selected for this illustration should be a combined third- and fourth-level one is consistent with the basic assumption stated in Chapter Three that effective long-term planning can be done only on these levels. But since this objective is part of an interacting system, it cannot be viewed in isolation. Of other third- and fourth-level objectives the one most relevant here is that of encouraging the liberalization trend in the Soviet Union by reinforcing the position of those leaders who believe coexistence to be possible and desirable. This is a vital objective and could be adversely affected by American policy toward Iran were that policy either so aggressive as to reinforce the view of Soviet hard liners that the United States cannot be lived with or so acquiescent that it reinforces the view, seemingly contradictory, of these same hard liners that American resistance is weak and would crumble under the impact of an assertive Soviet policy. Therefore, the ideal type American policy toward Iran will be designed to avoid either alarming or encouraging the ambitions of Soviet leaders.

Situational Analysis

For the ideal type policy, the core of the situational analysis is to be found in a description of those trends which have the greatest relevance in interstate relations. In the section that follows, the trends described will be categorized according to the scheme outlined in the ideal type model.

1) *Trends in power potential rating.* In most respects Iran's relative power potential is rising. Income from oil is by now very large and the rate of investments is high.[1] But in June, 1963, severe rioting occurred in Tehran. Estimates as to the number of casualties vary widely but the figure of 1,500 killed is not excessive. These two points illustrate very well both the assets and liabilities on the Iranian power ledger. Considering the dimensions of the rioting, the fact that the security forces held firm and were able to control the situation is of first significance. Quite clearly the Iranian army and security agency (SAVAK) are capable of maintaining internal order against a serious disturbance. This represents a substantial improvement in quality. On the other hand the riots reflected extreme dissatisfaction within Iran's urban middle and lower middle

---

1. In 1963 oil revenue was estimated at 130 million pounds as compared with 32.3 million pounds in 1955. Investments in the 1960–61 period equaled 58.5 million rials as compared with 17.1 million rials in 1955–56 (*Iran Almanac, 1963* [Tehran, 1964], pp. 253, 219).

classes and the religious and intellectual leadership and is indicative of a major power liability. The factor of morale is recognized as vital in the power potential ledger[2] and the political polarization demonstrated by the rioting suggests very low morale among the urban middle class. An extensive land reform program has been in effect since 1962 with the expressed purpose of attracting support for the regime from rural areas to offset the hostility in the urban areas. Government propagandists testify to the success of this program but independent evidence is lacking.[3] Considering the hostility of religious leaders to the regime and the prominence of religious leaders in rural Iran, there is reason to question the Shah's expectation of strong positive support from the peasantry.

A significant change since 1962 is also to be found in the improvement in quality of administration. In this period there has been an overflow of outstanding young administrators from the Iranian Plan Organization into leadership positions throughout the government, political as well as bureaucratic.

A summary of the trends in this category is the following:

a. A broadening industrial base, increasing investments and increasing oil revenues.

b. Increasing political polarization of the community with a concomitant decline of morale in urban areas.

c. Improving quality of leadership and discipline of the 200,000-man army and of SAVAK.

d. An apparently improving peasant morale.

e. A rapid improvement in the quality of bureaucratic leadership and in the quality of administration.

2) *Trends producing or discouraging mass participation in the government.* The picture that emerges here is a clear one. One of

2. Hans Morgenthau, *Politics Among Nations,* 3d ed. (New York, 1960), pp. 133–39.

3. For a well-informed picture of Iran's land reform program see Hossein Mahdavy, "The Coming Crisis in Iran," *Foreign Affairs,* October 1965, pp. 134–46.

the most obvious and significant developments in Iran is the rapid extension of political awareness into a previously politically inert peasantry and laboring group. Education is steadily expanding as is the communication network. This results in opportunities for upward mobility, which are increasingly recognized. With education and with a movement into urban centers comes an ability to comprehend Iran as a nation and to react to international stimuli.

The picture has two sides, however, and the other side counteracts to a considerable degree the trends for participation. Control of the press; rigging of elections; jailing, threatening, and even executing opposition leaders including religious leaders all characterize the present regime. Furthermore there is a clear trend toward an increase of repression. Since the voices of many of the natural leaders of the politically awakening mass are forcibly stilled, the mobilization process is retarded to a considerable degree. The overall effect is an increase in potential for political participation but a decrease in opportunity for independent nonritualistic participation.

A summary of trends in this category is the following:

a. A steadily increasing percentage of the population being educated.

b. A slowly improving ability of residents of more distant villages to move around the country.

c. A rapidly increasing percentage of the population becoming aware of Iran as a nation, capable of reacting to international stimuli, and capable of perceiving the possibility of direct political participation.

d. Increasingly tight control of the press.

e. Increasing restrictions placed on the natural leaders of the newly awakened and of the opposition-inclined public.

f. Increasing apathy and political alienation within the opposition-inclined public.

3) *Trends in elite relationships: public, political, and bureaucratic.*

The trend picture in the area of elite relationships is also becoming a clear one. In the American newspaper image of Iran, the societal villain in Iran has long been the so-called feudal landowner. A commonly accepted view of Mohammad Reza Shah has been that of a courageous David assaulting a feudal Goliath and finally overcoming him. In fact, the political leadership in Iran from 1953 through 1960 consisted of a court-landowner alliance. That alliance, with virtually overt support from the United States, had overturned the middle class-based and liberal intellectual-led regime of Dr. Mohammad Mossadeq. Since the Mossadeq regime had attracted and retained even in defeat substantial support from the urban politically aware population, the successor regime was constantly threatened. Throughout the 1950's the Shah could not safely dispense with either American or landowner support. But by 1960 his position was sufficiently consolidated that he could begin to drop his less-compatible allies from the traditional community. After 1960 the beginnings of a break with the landowners occurred and since then the power position, though not necessarily the total wealth, of the landowning class has been in decline. In its place has come a new careerist class of security officers and young administrators. Intellectual and middle-class leaders were sporadically persecuted from 1953 until 1963, but with the improved quality of the security forces the government was able to inaugurate a much tougher control in January, 1963. This has been reflected in severe curtailment of the activities of known opposition leaders, imprisonment of the more energetic leaders, suppression of religio-political leaders, a staged referendum, rigged elections, and the inauguration of the formative single party. This represents a move toward totalitarianism and by Middle Eastern standards Iran may be approaching the point at which such a characterization would be valid. Certainly the direct control of the individual is increasing with the steady elimination of intermediate groups.

A summary of trends in this category is the following:

a. A steady decline of the power and prestige of traditional land-owning and tribal leaders.

b. An increasingly effective suppression of overt political activity by opposition intellectual and middle-class leaders.

c. An increasingly effective suppression of political activity by religious leaders.

d. A steady decline of power held by old style, religious-oriented commercial leaders located in the bazaar and organized in guilds.

e. The beginning of a decline in the government's reliance on street leaders to control labor and to produce city mobs for demonstrations.

f. A steady reduction of the power of military officers with either a traditional or Nationalist background.

g. A rapid increase of the power of professional-minded military officers and of those officers who have identified with the regime.

h. A rapid increase of the power of officers of SAVAK, who are beginning to replace street leaders and conservative religious leaders as the control instrument for urban working and lower middle-class elements and who are rapidly achieving a central position in controlling the organs of communication.

i. A rapid increase in power of careerist technocrats within the bureaucracy.

j. A rapid increase in the concentration of power in the hands of the Shah and the court.

4) *Trends in relevant sections of elite and mass value systems.* Alterations in Iranian value systems reflect accurately the political polarization of elite elements and the growth in skepticism regarding the possibility of incorporating the liberal democratic process in Iran. In the Mossadeq years of 1951–53 the governing Nationalist elite was generally committed to the proposition that the liberal democratic process could be incorporated into Iran. Since then,

the overthrow of the Mossadeq government and the demonstrated longevity of the authoritarian royal regime have been deeply disillusioning to those who believed in this possibility, especially since the liberal democratic United States was thought to have been responsible for both Mossadeq's overthrow and the Shah's longevity.

Along with the decline in attachment to liberal democratic values has come the virtual demise of the values of the landed aristocracy, which not long ago were dominant. Also reflecting the belief that little can be done about the current regime, however unpopular, has been a mass disinterest in political values other than those directly associated with personal material well-being and career success. In line with this mass response is a trend within the intellectual element that is a counterpoint to the polarization trend. Many young men whose education and position permit them to aspire to top bureaucratic positions have concluded that the prospects for the regime's longevity are so good that an accommodation with the regime is sensible both from a personal and a national interest point of view. Conversely, another section of this same element, despairing of any hope of a gradual change, is prepared to accept the communist offer of a popular front. To do so, however, it is necessary for them to rationalize that Stalinism is dead and that polycentrism makes possible a patriotic alliance with communists.

The growth in the percentage of the population being educated is producing opposed trends in the acceptance of religious values. For lower- and lower middle-class elements, who traditionally turn to religious leadership, an understanding of and devotion to religious principles seems to be rising. For those attending institutions of higher learning, however, the long-standing secular trend appears to be continuing.

A summary of trends in this category is the following:

a. A rapid decline in middle-class and intellectual circles of an attachment to the value of a monarchy.

b. Increasing acceptance in professional and intellectual circles of values associated with socialism and neutralism.

c. Increasing disillusionment within middle-class and intellectual circles with liberal democratic values.

d. A rapid increase in the attraction of students to communist values as defined in the polycentrist school.

e. A continuing steady decline in intellectual circles of attachments to religious values.

f. An increasing acceptance and understanding of religious values within urban lower- and lower middle-class elements.

g. An increasing attachment among westernized technocrats in the bureaucracy to the values of order, efficiency, stability, and professional competence.

h. A rapidly declining adherence of upper-class elements to the traditional values ascribed to the landed aristocracy.

i. A rising priority given by the mass to achievement and material values.

j. A steady increase among the peasantry and other elements loyal to the Shah of an attachment to the value of a monarchy.

k. A continued increase in the attachment to national values in all sections of the population.

5) *Trends in relevant sections of elite and mass perceptions.* The predominant attitude-determining perception in Iran is the increasing belief that barring revolutionary action the regime of the Shah is likely to be long-lived. For those who cannot identify with the Shah or who believe the Shah seeks to destroy their power position, the prospect of longevity is viewed with a despair that easily leads to withdrawal or to a decision to turn to extralegal means for overturning the regime. For those who identify with the Shah or see their power position enhanced, the prospect of longevity leads to the granting of greater support for the regime. In the former category are to be found traditional landowners and tribal chiefs, middle-class and intellectual leaders, and most religious leaders. In the

latter group are to be found members of the government service and, presumably, growing numbers of peasants. Lower- and lower middle-class elements are placed in an ambivalent position since they accept as their leaders the increasingly alienated religious leaders and yet also perceive that the opportunity for upward mobility is increasingly available.

The predominant attitude-determining perception in the realm of external affairs is the belief that the Soviet Union is mellowing and that the intensity of the Soviet-American struggle is declining. However, the Sino-Soviet dispute is believed to offer a new alternative to those wishing to attract outside support to combat Anglo-American imperialism. China's inability at present to exert much influence in Iran is recognized but so too is a rapidly growing Chinese potential for doing so. Of nearly equal importance is the perception that American foreign policy is totally wedded to the regime of the Shah. Together, these perceptions generate within opposition elements a continuing disenchantment with the United States, an increasing belief that the Soviet Union can be lived with, and an increasing interest in China. A comparable pro-American attitude does not exist among those who identify with the regime, largely because of the fact that acceptance of the regime by its more articulate supporters is due less to any positive devotion than to the view of it as an unhappy, but the only reasonable, alternative. These perceptions lead also to a belief that regional relations are of increasing concern to Iran since interest in the Middle East by the great powers has declined in intensity.

A summary of trends in this category is the following:

a. A crystallizing belief within all sectors of the population that the longevity of the regime is assured as long as the Shah remains alive and the security forces loyal.
b. An increasing acceptance by all sectors of the population that the Shah is the focus of all governmental power in Iran.

c. An increasing acceptance by most politically active members of the middle-class and intellectual elements of the view that no program of compromise with the Shah can be found.

d. An increasing acceptance by the Shah and his supporters that governmental control can approach the absolute.

e. An increasing belief within urban lower and middle classes that upward mobility is possible.

f. An increasing acceptance by lower- and lower middle-class elements of the view that religious leaders are dedicated to their interests.

g. An increasing acceptance by peasant elements of the belief that a better life is possible and that the Shah is interested in providing that better life.

h. An increasing acceptance by tribal chiefs and landowners of the view that the old quasi-feudal order is beyond recall.

i. An increasing acceptance by religious leaders of the view that the Shah and his entourage seek to destroy their power.

j. An increasing acceptance by all sectors of the view that the intensity of the Cold War is in decline and that the Soviet Union is mellowing.

k. An increasing acceptance by middle-class and intellectual elements of the view that the Anglo-American commitment to the Shah's regime is total.

l. A decline in the previously widely held view among middle-class and intellectual elements that the Shah is a puppet of Anglo-American imperialism.

m. An increasing acceptance by middle-class intellectual elements of the view that the United States is the senior partner in a diminishing western imperial control of Iran and that American actions in the Dominican Republic and South Vietnam are directly parallel to those in Iran.

n. A steady downgrading of the perceived importance of

CENTO, which middle-class and intellectual elements in particular continue to regard as an instrument of western imperialism.

o. An increasingly widespread view among all sectors of the population, but particularly widely held within middle-class and intellectual circles, that the intensity of the Soviet threat is declining.

p. An increasing acceptance among all informed sectors of the view that the Soviet Union is unlikely to side with any opposition element.

q. An increasing acceptance among all interested elements of the view that China is gaining power potential in the Middle East and may soon be able to help counter Anglo-American influence.

r. An increasing acceptance among Nationalist opposition elements of the view that Arab nationalists are fighting for a cause parallel to their own and can be helpful in Iran.

s. An increasing acceptance among royalist elements of the view that Arab nationalists in Iraq, Syria, and the United Arab Republic wish to see in Iran a regime resembling their own.

6) *Trends in relevant elite and mass attitudes.* Iranian attitudes that have relevance for American policy makers flow naturally from the values and perceptions outlined above. Middle-class and intellectual opposition groups, disillusioned with liberal democracy and convinced of the Shah's longevity, have reacted either by passive acquiescence or by an expressed but as yet undeveloped determination to resort to extralegal means. The once-dominant belief that the United States could be persuaded to pressure the Shah into compromising with the opposition has largely departed. American support of the Shah is too unbending for such an expectation to continue. Furthermore, the Shah is judged to have sufficient internal strength to survive even if American support were to be sharply reduced. Consequently the focus of attention has shifted from the

American community to the court itself. Along with this has come a crystallization of hostility toward the Shah personally. The Nationalist image of a future government controlled by them consists of a socialist, one-party dictatorship following a neutralist foreign policy.

The previously held belief of noncommunist middle-class and intellectual opposition groups that the withdrawal of American support for the Shah was their best hope of achieving power was in part responsible for their unwillingness to consider a popular front with the communist Tudeh Party and to solicit Soviet support. They believed that American policy could not be altered in their favor if there were any hint of communist infiltration. As expectations of American support evaporated, opposition to a popular front began to fade. But, ironically, by this time the Soviet Union was perceived to be far too conservative to give any real support. Chinese support, however, looms as a decreasingly distant possibility and pro-Chinese attitudes among noncommunist opposition groups, and especially students, are increasingly common.

Confronted with what appears to be a steady loss of influence, religious leaders of all philosophical persuasions are becoming hostile to the regime. In spite of their differences with the secular-minded Nationalists, these leaders are willing to enter into clandestine alliance with the Nationalists for the overthrow or fundamental alteration of the regime. Both religious leaders and Nationalists are quite willing to seek support from nationalistic Arab regimes for their purposes. The ability of the religious leaders to mobilize their following for political purposes was demonstrated by the rioting in June, 1963. But the futility of this type of resistance was also starkly revealed and the essentially anomic display of hostility and frustration is not likely to be repeated.

Attitudes among the careerist element in the bureaucracy and security forces vary from unenthusiastic accommodation to strong identfication. The Novin Iran Party, which appears to be designed to become a single-party control instrument, has attracted mainly careerist elements. Whereas there is no evidence of spontaneous enthusiasm from this group, there is a clearly reflected attitude that the regime is beneficial both to the individual party member and to the community. This attitude differs sharply from that of the members of the government-ordained parties of the late 1950's, the Mardom and Melliyun. Attitudes toward these parties had a farcical undertone, which prevented their being taken very seriously.

The element of the population that has been most vigorously wooed by the regime since 1961 is the peasantry. There are surface indications that the land distribution program has indeed attracted support and has reinforced an ancient propensity to look upon the institution of the monarchy with awe and respect. However, the ultimate goal of the land reform program as outlined by the former Minister of Agriculture, Hassan Arsenjani, is to create an attitude on the part of the peasantry that can produce positive and effective support in the political area.[4] The purpose is to counter the popular antipathy to be found among the urban middle class and the urban lower and lower middle classes who are influenced by religious leaders. Standing as obstacles here, assuming the anything but assured physical success of the program, are the narrowness of the political horizons of the peasant and his custom of looking to his religious leader for guidance in both political and social matters. He may look with favor on the vague father image of the Shah but will be bewildered by the complex political machinations in Tehran. Furthermore if the trend among religious leaders continues to be unfavorable for the Shah the peasantry may be led away from their traditional support for the monarchy. The program has surely had some at least temporary beneficial results for the regime but there is nothing to indicate that a widely pervasive change in attitude would bring the peasants into positive defense of the regime.

A summary of trends in this category is the following:

4. *The New York Times,* July 29, 1961, p. 13.

a. An increasing hostility to the United States among opposition middle-class and intellectual elements.

b. An increasing disillusionment among opposition elements with the Soviet Union because of its pro-regime attitude but a simultaneously decreasing hostility to the proposition of seeking Soviet support.

c. An increasing receptivity among opposition elements to the proposal of establishing a popular front with the Tudeh Party.

d. An increasing willingness of opposition elements to turn ultimately to China for support against the regime and an intensifying identification with the Chinese in world affairs.

e. A decreasing interest among opposition leaders in pursuing as a central strategic objective an alteration of American foreign policy toward Iran.

f. A decreasing willingness of opposition activists to consider any accommodation with the Shah.

g. An increasing dissatisfaction among opposition elements with moderate, accommodationist leaders.

h. An increasing readiness on the part of opposition activists to turn to direct clandestine political and parliamentary action.

i. An increasing interest on the part of opposition leaders in exploring the potential support from nationalist Arab regimes in Iraq, Syria, and the United Arab Republic.

j. An increasing determination on the part of opposition leaders to pursue a policy of neutrality should they come to power.

k. An increasing acceptance by opposition leaders of the proposition that a liberal democratic regime cannot again be established in mid-twentieth-century Iran, and an increasing acceptance of the necessity to establish a single-party, socialist, authoritarian regime.

l. An increasing willingness of opposition leaders to form an effective clandestine alliance with religious leaders.

m. A decreasing interest on the part of middle-class and intellectual elements generally in politics and a resultant increase in passivity.

n. An increasing hostility toward the regime of religious leaders generally.

o. An increasing willingness of all but the most conservative religious leaders to furnish political leadership for the urban lower and lower middle classes.

p. An increasing willingness of the urban lower and lower middle classes to follow the political leadership of religious leaders and a decreasing willingness to follow government-employed street leaders.

q. An increasing receptivity for the Tudeh Party and its program, especially among university students studying in Europe.

r. A decreasing interest on the part of upper-class politicians in any effort to alter the political system.

s. An increasing explicit support for the Shah from elements of the peasantry.

t. An increasing willingness of the technocrats of the bureaucracy to grant implicit support to the regime.

u. An increasing willingness of one section of the technocrats to grant explicit and enthusiastic support to the regime and to institutionalize this support in the form of a single pro-government party.

v. An increasing enthusiasm for the regime from SAVAK officers and from army officers of lower middle-class origin, who credit the regime with their improved social status.

w. An increasing willingness of the regime to resort to terroristic control mechanisms.

Determining Capability

In the ideal type model the leverage system that operates between two states is constructed as a means of translating strategic interaction into influence terms. Since the United States–Iran leverage system was constructed and described in Chapter Two it will only be summarized here.

1. Passive levers
   a. Awareness of interdependence for defense
   b. Perceived economic and political instability
   c. Perceived irrationality and irresponsibility of leadership
   d. Perceived public attitudes
2. Active levers
   a. Perceived ability to grant or withhold economic, technical, and military aid
   b. Perceived vulnerability to exploitation of domestic political dissatisfaction
   c. Perceived willingness to alter the type of relationship

Objectives in Terms of Trend Manipulation

In order to achieve the objective of containing the Soviet Union, the United States has since 1946 pursued the goal of a noncommunist and stable Iranian government capable of resisting Soviet-backed subversion efforts. In the early Dulles years there was in addition the vigorously pursued goal of constructing military alliances in Asia that would deter direct invasion from communist states. Iran with its vital strategic location was central to the success of this goal. But later, as direct invasion was perceived to be less and less likely and in any case to be deterred primarily through developing thermonuclear warfare capabilities, military assistance to Iran was viewed essentially as a means for helping the regime achieve internal stability.

Taking this real American objective and incorporating it into the ideal type model calls for a translation in terms of trend alteration. This leads quickly to the discovery of the basic dilemma of American policy toward Iran. In the category of trends involving the power potential of Iran, all but one are favorable to American objectives. The United States government wishes to see an Iran with an expanding economic base, a security force capable of maintaining order, an improving administration, and an ever-broadening base of support from the peasantry. Therefore American policy should merely encourage these long-term trends. It will be some time, however, before the government can count on really positive support from the peasantry even if the current trend continues and, as was seen, this is doubtful. In the meantime the alienation of or lack of support from middle-class, intellectual, and religious elements in urban areas is a distinct threat to the stability of Iran. The Iranian security forces have demonstrated that they can put down even severe rioting, but stability in Iran rests on the continued presence and leadership of the Shah. Were he to die, be assassinated, or abdicate, the possibility of chaos or even a rapid move into the Soviet or Chinese orbit cannot be discounted. Therefore a basic American policy objective should be to alter or reverse the trend working for the polarization of the Iranian community.

What this amounts to in more specific terms is a need to seek the reversal of several of the strong attitudinal trends which were outlined above. Central among these trends is a growing dissatisfaction among opposition elements with moderate and accommodationist leaders. This is symptomatic of a willingness to turn to direct action and an attitude of total opposition to the Shah. The joining in this attitude of religio-political leaders and the willingness of the secular and religious opposition leaders to work together in total opposition underlines the basic threat to the regime's stability.

Another series of trends, closely related to the above, is also clearly detrimental to American objectives in Iran. For many years opposition elements believed that the United States had been deceived into adopting a policy of hostility toward Dr. Mossadeq by a clever and unscrupulous British diplomacy. Soviet propaganda prior to, during, and since the Mossadeq regime has advanced the theme that in fact the United States is the senior partner in Anglo-American imperial control of Iran and the Middle East generally.

American policy in the Dominican Republic and in Southeast Asia has complemented the Soviet propaganda theme for the Iranian opposition. As mentioned above, these Iranians identify both policies with the 1953 American decision to help overthrow Dr. Mossadeq. In their eyes American policy, with the brief hiatus of the Kennedy years, has been consistently in opposition to popular movements. A survey of the Iranian opposition press published abroad indicates that the Iranian opposition is increasingly convinced that the United States is indeed the senior partner in the western alliance and that the contention can no longer be made that a clever British diplomacy has deceived the Americans.[5]

Coincidentally, and probably related to this loss of hope that American policy will return to a support of Iranian nationalism, is the increasing attraction for Iranian students of the communist ideological blueprint. Evidence for this conclusion is to be found in the increasing strength of communist elements in the annual conference of Iranian students' associations in Europe. Attitudinal trends related to these changes in perception and value attraction are damaging to American objectives. Opposition newspapers and student associations outside Iran reflect an increasing hostility to the United States. Coincidentally there is a marked increase in student expression of support for a popular front with the Tudeh.[6] Less noticeable are arguments in favor of seeking Soviet assistance, although these too appear to be on the increase. Were there not a simultaneously increasing disillusionment with the Soviet Union due to its friendly policy toward the Iranian regime, this trend would probably move much more rapidly. The advisability of soliciting Chinese backing is gaining increasing support but the trend is relatively sluggish because of the view that Chinese

5. Newspapers in this survey included *Daneshjoo, Bulletin Jebhe Melli Iran, Iran Azad, Bakhtar Emruz, Andishe Iran.*

6. This conclusion has been reached as a result of private conversations with a large number of Iranian students studying in the United States.

capability in Iran is only slight and is likely to remain so for several years to come. Quite clearly American objectives in Iran, when spelled out in terms of trend manipulation, call for reversing these attitudinal trends except for the increasing disillusionment with the Soviet Union.

Were it possible to deal with each trend in isolation, the dilemma of American policy in Iran would not be a serious one. But even on the general objectives level one serious contradiction manifests itself. The conclusion was drawn that the trend toward an increasingly effective internal security force was obviously favorable to American objectives and therefore should be reinforced. The further conclusion was drawn that those trends moving Iran in a direction of political polarization and leading opposition elements to look with more favor on a popular front with the communists should be reversed. However, the Iranian security forces, and SAVAK in particular, have become a symbol of the authoritarian control that is continuing to alienate middle-class, intellectual, and religious elements. The dislike of the security force is so intense that a reversal of these latter trends is unlikely if the trend toward an increasingly effective security force continues. Therefore, the American policy maker is confronted from the beginning with a fundamental policy choice. He can direct what influence the United States possesses toward a continuance of the trend toward an efficient terror control instrument. But if he makes this choice he must accept a tightly bipolarized polity for some time to come until long-range labor, administrative, and land reform projects bear fruit in the form of a broader base of support. Or he can seek to alter the security forces in policy and composition in order to reduce the hostility of the noncommunist opposition. But if he makes this choice he runs the risk common to all who seek to weaken a hated terror control instrument: the very real possibility that the situation will rapidly get out of control.

As summarized here the two policy alternatives appear to be

roughly equal in terms of risk involved and the likelihood of achieving the general objective. If this were true the policy maker would likely opt for the status quo. But a basic situational factor has been ignored. Iranian stability today rests on the continued presence of the Shah in power and the Shah is mortal. Furthermore no one can be confident that labor and agricultural reform will in fact have the long-term result of mobilizing the laboring and agricultural population in support of the Shah. And even were this result a certainty in the long run, the short-run danger of the loss of Iran to the West in parallel fashion to that of Iraq in 1958, when a dictator allied to the West was overthrown, remains a grim one. The ideal policy, therefore, will focus on reducing polarization as the basic American objective in Iran. Since polarization cannot be reduced without inaugurating changes in the security forces the trend toward an increasingly effective security force must be altered. This calls for an American policy directed toward encouraging the growth of an effective internal security force that is acceptable to noncommunist opposition elements.

Objectives and Capability

American technical and military support of the Iranian regime is and has been substantial, and American diplomatic support for the regime approaches that of total commitment. Therefore, the American impact on Iranian trend developments has been and certainly will continue to be extremely significant. The confusion surrounding the concept of interference is such that this type of trend influence is not generally regarded by the American interested public as interference simply because American material, diplomatic, and psychological support of the regime has been solicited by the Iranian government. In the eyes of the various opposition elements, however, American policy is one of gross interference in Iranian affairs. Nevertheless, from the point of view of capability, there is a substantial difference between interference in the form of strengthening trends perceived by the regime to be favorable and interference in the form of altering or reversing trends the regime perceives to be favorable.

In this regard American trend influence in Iran can be placed in three categories: the influencing of trends in a direction welcomed by the regime, the influencing of trends in a direction viewed by the regime as generally favorable but about which there is some ambivalence and differing opinions, and the influencing of trends in a direction viewed by the regime as in sum, to one degree or another, damaging to its interests. Since August, 1953, the impact of American policy has been quite substantial in influencing trends in a direction viewed by the regime as favorable and virtually non-existent in influencing trends in a direction viewed as unfavorable. There has been some effort to influence trends in a direction that some Iranian officials regarded as dangerous, but this effort has generally been in the area of economic policy and those elements resisting the policy have rarely been in tune with the Shah's stated plans for his country. American policy has not been all the Shah would have wished. Indeed on many occasions his disappointment has been expressed emphatically.[7] But the fact remains that the United States government has at no time attempted to pressure the Shah into accepting policies that run counter to his long-term projection of an Iran under the benevolent but firm control of the Pahlavi dynasty.

It is impossible to say without access to government files whether the failure to place pressure on the Iranian regime to alter basic and long-range policy objectives was because of a lack of capability to do so. But a glance at the American-Iranian leverage system would suggest that American capabilities for persuading the regime to

7. Amir Assadolah Alam, upon resigning, gave as his reason the "tardy and insufficient" American aid to his government (*The New York Times,* March 8, 1964, p. 8). His predecessor, Ali Amini, had made a similar remark when he resigned (*ibid.,* July 19, 1962, p. 26).

alter its course are at best limited. As long as American policy calls for a stable and noncommunist Iran and American policy makers are convinced that only the Shah can provide such an Iran, the American leverage position will remain a weak one. The question that needs to be answered is, does the United States have the leverage strength to persuade the Shah to work for an immediate broadening of the base of support of his regime?

Potentially the strongest American lever in the Iranian-American leverage system is Iran's awareness of interdependence with the United States for defense. But this lever can be developed only if the Iranians perceive a likelihood of a basic alteration in American Cold War strategy. There is some evidence that, in fact, the Iranians do believe that the Soviet coexistence policy of Khrushchev and his successors is altering basic American strategy with a downgrading of the CENTO powers.[8] But Iranian actions argue that the regime continues to see the United States as heavily committed in Iran. The remaining two favorable levers are the Iranian perception of American public attitudes toward Iran, and the Iranian perception of an American ability to exploit Iranian political dissatisfaction. The strength of the first of these levers, however, is questionable. Should the American public as a result of unfavorable publicity become hostile to the authoritarian nature of the Iranian regime, the government would indeed be granted a strong lever. The argument could be made that the American government's ability to give full support to the Iranian regime is contingent on support from the American public manifested through Congress. Public approval, in turn, is unlikely unless the regime engages in political reform. However, for the American government to stimulate public attitudes of this nature would run counter to American traditions and American values. This lever, therefore, will become available only if a public

8. This is reflected in vastly improved U.S.S.R.-Iranian relations and a greater emphasis on intraregional concerns.

reaction develops independently. In fact, not only are American officials not seeking to generate such a public response, they have taken steps to remove from this country Iranians who, if they were successful in reaching the communications media, might produce such a popular response.[9]

There remains only the perceived American ability to exploit Iranian political dissatisfaction. As the attitudinal trends suggest, the potential of this lever is in rapid decline. Earlier efforts of the noncommunist opposition to persuade the United States to alter its policy[10] had failed so completely that the opposition leaders and, even more, the rank and file have given up hope. Still there remains a strong possibility that the opposition would welcome any American overtures on its behalf. And the past behavior of the Shah[11] demonstrates a great sensitivity to this possibility.

Therefore the potential for adding to the leverage strength of the perceived ability to exploit the Iranian political dissatisfaction remains strong. What is called for are some concrete manifestations of interest on the part of Americans, official or nonofficial, in the National Front as an alternative noncommunist regime. However this lever is only part of the system. An alteration of its strength would result in an alteration of the entire Iranian-American leverage system. Almost certainly countering the added strength of the above lever would be an addition to the leverage strength of perceived Iranian willingness to alter the relationship. This additional strength would be derived from the perceived irrationality of the Iranian leadership. Although it is true that the Iranian regime desperately needs American assistance, the Shah personally does not. He could easily depart from Iran for a relaxed and luxurious life on the

9. See the example of Ali Fatemi above.

10. Richard W. Cottam, *Nationalism in Iran* (Pittsburgh, Pa., 1964), pp. 234–36.

11. *Ibid.*

Riviera and he has demonstrated before that this alternative is well in mind. His hints of abdication or of leaving CENTO therefore would and should be taken seriously in Washington. Furthermore the Shah also has the capability now of responding to American overtures to the National Front by arresting the entire National Front leadership. Were he to do this the only American recourse would be to threaten a basic alteration of strategy, and building credibility for such a threat would indeed be difficult. Containing the Soviet Union in the Middle East is too vital an element of perceived American strategy.

Consequently the American ability to develop the lever of perceived ability to exploit Iranian domestic political dissatisfaction is much narrower than a first glance would indicate. In South Vietnam the American government has on more than one occasion been in the unhappy position of threatening a basic alteration of strategy. In the Middle East such threats would have even less credibility. Therefore, the reluctance of the American government to seek to improve its leverage position in a situation such as that of Iranian-American relations is thoroughly understandable.

The conclusion might well be drawn at this point that in a dependent relationship the state with the higher power potential rating will be incapable of placing really significant pressure on the state with the lower rating unless it can convincingly threaten a basic alteration of strategy. At least until recently the Soviet Union in its dependent relationships could in an ultimate bargaining confrontation threaten a conventional armed attack. But such an American threat in Iran would have no credibility. Nevertheless there is serious reason for questioning the validity of this conclusion. There is a basic fallacy behind the listing of two or three policy alternatives in a given foreign policy situation. The fallacy lies in the implicit assumption that only gross alternatives such as the following are available: If the Shah is to be backed then the backing must be 100 per cent; or if the conclusion is drawn that the present trends are leading toward a likely communist takeover, then support must be withdrawn and the Shah replaced by an alternative regime. The ideal type approach suggests on the contrary that there is a multitude of alternative tactical schemes and that the risks involved in following either of the two gross alternatives are unnecessary.

The conclusion to be drawn from exploring the possibility of adding to the leverage strength of a perceived American ability to exploit domestic political dissatisfaction is not that leverage strength cannot be added. Rather the conclusion is that additional leverage strength to be gained here is limited at present. Concrete manifestations of interest in National Front elements must be sufficiently indirect to leave the government leaders in serious doubt as to their significance. In fact a major area for diplomatic probing is precisely at this point. The Shah gives every sign of wanting to remain in office and to be succeeded by his son. It is unlikely that anything short of a severe provocation would lead him to seriously threaten to abdicate. Obviously there is room for maneuvering and the object of probing would be to determine how much room does in fact exist.

Constructing a Strategy

What is called for in this section of the ideal foreign policy is to spell out the general objectives in terms of desired trend alterations. Following from the above discussion of capability, the strategy will be outlined on three levels in descending order of priority. The first-level strategy is designed to add to American leverage strength for the achievement of the objective. The second level will be directed toward the central task of reducing political polarization. The third level will be concerned with preventing the loss of Iranian governmental control in the transitional period.

The conclusion was reached above that in order to add to American capability the most promising possibility is to seek to increase the leverage strength of the perceived American ability to exploit domestic political dissatisfaction. Two trends, one perceptual and the other attitudinal, which were outlined above have been acting to reduce the strength of this lever. These are:

5k. an increasing acceptance by middle-class and intellectual elements of the view that the Anglo-American commitment to the Shah's regime is total, and

6e. a decreasing interest among opposition leaders in pursuing as a central strategic objective an alteration of American foreign policy toward Iran.

As these trends progress the regime will perceive that the American ability to exploit domestic political dissatisfaction is declining. Therefore an implicit American threat to turn to the opposition is increasingly likely to be disregarded. What is called for is not a reversal of these trends, a development which might well produce the feared threat of abdication, but rather an alteration of each. The direction of alteration should be toward a belief that, whereas the Americans are committed to keeping the Shah on his throne, they are also anxious to see him make a determined effort to work with the opposition. This change in perceptual direction could, in turn, indicate to opposition leaders that, whereas outright American support for their cause is most unlikely, American support for their being included in a future government is possible and should be solicited. These trend alterations should add to American leverage strength.

The primary trend target of the second level of strategy would be the removal of:

1c. increasing political polarization of the community with a concomitant decline of morale in urban areas.

To accomplish this task an assault is necessary on a number of trends in the categories of elite relationships, mass and elite values, perceptions, and attitudes. Regarding elite relationships the relevant trends are:

3b. an increasingly effective suppression of overt political activity by opposition intellectual and middle-class leaders,

3c. an increasingly effective suppression of political activity by religious leaders,

3f. a steady reduction in power of military officers with either a traditional or Nationalist background, and

3j. a rapid increase in the concentration of power in the hands of the Shah and the court.

The first two trends are, of course, reflective of and central to the polarization process. Any major effort to reduce polarization calls for their reversal. To the extent that the trend in *3f* represents a development in professionalism of the armed forces, there is no necessity to reverse the trend. Clear discrimination against men from upper-class or middle-class families who are unhappy with the regime should be discouraged however. This trend should be altered therefore in a direction of nondiscriminatory recruiting and promoting. Quite obviously trend *3j* must be reversed if polarization is to be reduced. But here the speed of reduction of the Shah's power is the vital factor, and no point is more essential than the conclusion that this be a very slow process. Otherwise the fact of polarization could produce an explosion.

The trend in the category of elite/mass values that is relevant at this level is:

4a. a rapid decline in middle-class and intellectual circles of an attachment to the value of a monarchy.

This trend needs to be reversed in any strategic plan for providing noncommunist stability in Iran. There is no reason to conclude that American interests call for a permanent attachment to the institution of the monarchy in Iran. But given the existing polarization in the country and the very real probability that a sudden removal of the Shah could produce serious instability, the perpetuation of the institution of the monarchy until the polarization has been significantly reduced is a strategic requirement.

In the area of elite/mass perceptions the affected trends would be:

5c. an increasing acceptance by most politically active members of the middle-class and intellectual elements of the view that no program of compromise with the Shah can be found,

5d. an increasing acceptance by the Shah and his supporters of the view that governmental control can approach the absolute, and

5l. a decline in the previously widely held view among middle-class and intellectual elements that the Shah is a puppet of Anglo-American imperialism.

That the first two trends should be reversed is obviously in tune with American strategic requirements. The third trend should be reinforced. Thus far American encouragement for this trend has been inadvertent. For many years opposition Iranians sought to interpret various Iranian government policies as being in tune with American interests and therefore of American sponsorship.[12] But this type of reasoning has become increasingly strained, especially since clear evidence of significant Iranian-American disagreements has occasionally emerged.[13] Therefore there is an increasing acceptance of a conclusion that in most areas of decision making the Shah is his own agent. Although this trend is resulting in an increase in hostility directed toward the Shah personally, it is adding to the American potential for maneuverability. Tactical development of this strategic conclusion therefore should include a conscious policy of strengthening and accelerating this trend.

Finally in the area of elite/mass attitudes the relevant trends are:

12. *Ibid.,* pp. 230–36, 303–04, 318–19.
13. See *ibid.,* p. 305, for an instance in which this disagreement has come to the surface.

6f. a decreasing willingness of opposition activists to consider any accommodation with the Shah,

6g. an increasing dissatisfaction among opposition elements with moderate, accommodationist leaders,

6h. an increasing readiness on the part of opposition activists to turn to direct clandestine political and paramilitary action,

6l. an increasing willingness of opposition leaders to form an effective clandestine alliance with religious leaders generally,

6n. an increasing hostility toward the regime of religious leaders generally,

6o. an increasing willingness of all but the most conservative religious leaders to furnish political leadership for the urban lower and lower middle classes, and

6w. an increasing willingness of the regime to resort to terroristic control mechanisms.

The first six of these trends reflect attitudes of opposition elements that are working toward an ever-tightening polarization. They should be reversed. The final trend is indicative of the regime's conclusion that the opposition can be controlled by force and that compromise need not be considered. This trend too should be reversed.

The above trend alterations together constitute the central strategic task of the ideal American foreign policy toward Iran. They add up to a concerted attack on political polarization in Iran. What is called for implicitly is a liberalization program whose key element is a downgrading of the power position of the security forces. Such a program involves serious risks. Much of the basis for the stability of the regime has rested on the efficiency of the security forces as a control instrument. Another mainstay of the regime has been the popular Iranian belief that the Anglo-American influence in Iranian domestic politics is decisive and that the Anglo-American commitment to the regime has been total. The strategy outlined above would weaken both of these elements of strength for the regime. As a consequence the danger inherent in all such liberalization programs will manifest itself—the weakening of control will produce a revolutionary upheaval. Therefore a third level of strategy must be concerned with maintaining the strength, or the ability to influence, of two major control instruments, the bureaucratic system and the security forces.

The two primary trends to be achieved at this level are the following:

1b. improving quality of leadership and discipline of the 200,000-man army and of SAVAK, and

1e. a rapid improvement in the quality of bureaucratic leadership and in the quality of administration.

Both of these trends are favorable for the achievement of the specified strategic ends but both are likely to be affected adversely by any tactical scheme devised simply to produce the trend alteration in the second level of strategy. Therefore the tactical scheme adopted should take into account both the necessity for achieving the second-level strategic ends and also for maintaining these two trends.

Spelled out in terms of elite relationship trends, the following should be considered:

3g. a rapid increase in power of professional-minded officers and of those officers who have identified with the regime,

3h. a rapid increase in power of officers of SAVAK who are beginning to replace street leaders and conservative religious leaders as the control instrument for urban working- and lower middle-class elements and who are rapidly achieving a central position in control of the organs of communication, and

3i. a rapid increase in power of careerist technocrats within the bureaucracy.

These trends include one element that is very favorable for the long-term achievement of noncommunist stability in Iran—the growth of professionalism in both the security forces and the bureaucracy. Since this professionalization involves a general willingness to serve the government loyally, the new Iranian professional can be classified as at least having accommodated to the regime. In a polarized society professional neutrality is far too subtle a point to be granted. Consequently for those in the opposition pole the professional is part of the enemy camp. To the extent that the opposition continues to identify the regime with western imperialism this leads to questioning the very patriotism of the professionals. Were a sudden upheaval to occur the professional officer and bureaucrat might easily go under with the court. The ideal strategy here calls for the continuation of the professionalization trend even in the face of an attempt to reduce the polarization.

The assumption above is that hostility to the professional among opposition elements is not so intense as to preclude any general rapprochement. The argument for this assumption is based partly on the fact that a great many of the younger technicians and the younger opposition leaders were educated together and come from the same middle- to upper middle-class family background. They are, therefore, friends and relatives. But the other element considered in these trends, military and SAVAK officers, who actively identify with the regime, are more likely to be of lower middle-class origin. Hostility to this element within the opposition is intense to the point of irreconcilability. It is therefore unlikely that any serious effort could be made toward reducing polarization in Iran unless the trend toward an increase in power of this group were reversed. In the interest of short-term stability, however, this cannot be done in any drastic manner. A simple reversal of the trend and a very gradual downgrading of this element is what is called for. Admittedly, if this were to occur the long-term prospects for these officers would not be good and one of the major risks of this strategy, and one that must be probed, is the possibility of their resorting to direct action.

In the area of mass and elite values only one is of significant concern to this strategic level. That is:

4g. an increasing attachment among westernized technocrats in the bureaucracy to the values of order, efficiency, stability, and professional competence.

In view of the previous discussion, the ideal strategy calls for encouraging this trend.

Regarding mass and elite perceptions again one trend is directly relevant. That is:

5a. a crystallizing perception within all sectors of the population that the longevity of the regime is assured as long as the Shah remains alive and the security forces loyal.

This trend could easily be among the first casualties of the second-level strategy. Were this to occur, the possibility of a rapid deterioration of control would be a real one. Therefore it is vital that at the same time when the Shah accepts a downgrading of his own position of influence the population should not perceive his actions as a prelude to abdication or overthrow. This trend therefore should be maintained.

In the area of mass and elite attitudes the relevant trends closely parallel those concerning elite relationships. They are:

6t. an increasing willingness of the technocrats of the bureaucracy to grant implicit support to the regime,

6u. an increasing willingness of one section of the technocrats to grant explicit and enthusiastic support to the regime and to institutionalize this support in the form of a single pro-government party, and

6v. an increasing enthusiasm for the regime from SAVAK officers and from army officers of lower middle-class origin who credit the regime with their improved social status.

Since holding the bureaucracy together is a short-term necessity for this period, continued support for the regime from technocrats and security force officers is essential. The impact of the strategy as described here, however, would be such that at least disillusionment and waning enthusiasm could be anticipated. The specific strategic objective here would be to accept the reversal of trends *6u* and *6v* but to maintain sufficient support for the regime to prevent either a collapse of authority or a turning to direct action. From a long-term point of view the maintenance of trend *6t* is important since a competent and professional bureaucracy is necessary for long-term stability.

Little has been said in the second and third levels of trends concerning values, perceptions, and attitudes that relate to Iran's foreign policy. Reinforcing trend *5l,* which described a decreasing tendency to regard the Shah as an agent of Anglo-American imperialism, was called for. But no others were mentioned. The reason for this neglect is the conclusion that the trends in foreign policy values, perceptions, and attitudes that are harmful to American objectives are the result of the perceived totality of the American commitment to the regime. Since the strategy outlined above would lead to a serious questioning of the totality of this commitment a reversal of the concerned trends could be anticipated. This reversal would be generally beneficial and no further American effort here should be necessary. Some of the relevant trends here are the following:

4d. a rapid increase in the attraction of students to communist values as defined in the polycentrist school,

5m. an increasing acceptance by middle-class and intellectual elements of the view that the United States is the senior partner in a diminishing western imperial control of Iran,

6a. an increasing hostility among opposition middle-class and intellectual elements to the United States,

6c. an increasing receptivity among opposition elements to the proposal of establishing a popular front with the Tudeh Party, and

6q. an increasing receptivity for the Tudeh Party and its program, especially among university students studying in Europe.

Tactical Planning: The Diplomatic Probe

As stated in the previous chapter, the situational analysis even under the best conditions must be viewed in all of its particulars as tentative. Statements of trends should be based on supporting evidence but only rarely will this evidence be conclusive. They must, therefore, be regarded as assertions whose validity is yet to be tested. The same is true of the leverage system as constructed. The next step in the ideal foreign policy therefore is to identify the levers and trends most in need of verification. Following this, policy-independent probes should be constructed for those trends and levers for which some verification is necessary before any tactical scheme is finally adopted.

Based on a review of the situational analysis and capability determination the conclusion is that the following questions must be probed either prior to the construction of a tactical plan or in the early stages of execution of the tactical plan:

1) How much and what kinds of pressure can be placed on the Shah without running a serious risk of his abdicating?

2) Would the Shah be willing to accept a reduction in his power which he may perceive as possibly leading eventually to his becoming in fact a constitutional monarch?

3) Does the Nationalist opposition believe that the American policy, which is perceived to be one of the total support for the Shah, is alterable?

4) Is a return by the Nationalists to their previous tactical goal of seeking to alter American policy toward Iran possible?

5) Have Tudeh efforts to form a popular front produced enough converts among the Nationalists to prevent a move toward accommodation with the West?

6) Are the moderate and essentially liberal National Front leaders still capable of controlling the movement?

7) Is it possible to revive the previous Nationalist attitude that they could endorse the Shah as a constitutional monarch?

8) Is it possible to revive the previous willingness of antiregime religious leaders to endorse the Shah as a constitutional monarch?

9) Is the National Front capable of formulating and supporting a constructive economic and social development program that is specific, phased, and workable?

10) Is the National Front willing to abide by the essence of the oil agreement?

11) Could a more popularly based regime remain in CENTO?

12) Could the National Front accept the professional core of the bureaucracy and army officers as politically neutral and not the agents of a particular regime?

13) Would a move toward accommodation with the Nationalist opposition seriously damage the morale of the supporters of the regime?

14) Would this move toward accommodation seriously weaken the ability of the security forces to maintain order?

15) Is the landowning element in fact so weak that a relaxation of control would not permit a serious effort to overturn the government?

16) Would the initiation of the above strategic scheme result in an alteration of Soviet and Chinese strategy and tactics?

17) Would the initiation of the above strategic scheme seriously affect United States relations with Turkey?

18) Would the British be sympathetic to the above strategic scheme to the point of being willing to engage in joint tactical planning?

Reasonably persuasive answers must be gained for the first four questions before a tactical plan can be constructed. The assumption that the Shah would tolerate the application of some pressure and would agree to give up very gradually some of his power prerogatives is basic to the situational analysis. If it were discovered that the Shah would respond to the slightest hint of American interest in the Nationalists by abdicating or by launching a severely repressive campaign against the Nationalists, then obviously American capability vis-à-vis Iran would be weak. Likewise, if it were discovered that the National Front was irreconcilably hostile to any consideration of cooperation with the United States, American leverage capability in Iran would be weak. Either discovery would necessitate a reevaluation of the Iranian-American leverage system construct and an alteration of the trend analysis. The strategy as devised would have to be abandoned.

In fact enough is known at the outset to make either of the above eventualities most unlikely. The Shah gives every indication of wishing to remain fully in power. Furthermore he is much too aware of and pleased with his image as a reform-minded progressive monarch to turn lightly to severe repressions of a noncommunist opposition.[14] At the same time, the Nationalists continue to make efforts to persuade the American public that their government's policy in Iran is both immoral and short-sighted.[15] The question therefore is really one of establishing a better estimate of the range of maneuverability available to the American government. It can hardly be denied that some maneuverability does exist.

Both the number and variety of probes that could be devised here are great. The three-phased probe described below is designed as much to illustrate the use of these three types of probes as to

14. See *Ibid.,* pp. 297–301, for an instance of this point. However since January, 1963, he has been less inhibited.

15. The Iranian Student Organization in the United States has been increasingly active in this regard. In April, 1965, a conference stimulated by that group was held at Harvard University partly for this purpose.

indicate how answers to the questions can be gained. To begin with, a probe utilizing the American press has been selected. In Chapter Three the point was made that a use of the American press to the extent that it could be considered "managed" raises important questions of value that should not be evaded by government, journalists, or the attentive public. There will certainly be readers who will regard the use of the press to be described below as beyond the bounds of acceptability. However, so long as journalists use government officials as sources there is the chance that these sources will try to use the reporters to enhance their bureaucratic goals. Whether the press can be accurately described as "managed" depends in the last analysis on the attitude and the competence of the journalists involved.

This aspect of the probe in Iran is made possible by the general inadequacy of American press reporting of Iran. Ever since the much-heralded inauguration of a major land reform program, the American press has seemed to treat the Iranian regime as sacrosanct. The jailing of the entire leadership of the National Front in January, 1963, was hardly noted, and when in January, 1963, a referendum on a government reform program produced over 99 per cent approval there was no suggestion that a little managing might have been involved.[16] The failure of the American press to note the intense hostility to the regime in Iran, especially the incredibly inadequate coverage of the 1963 riots, has a good deal to do with the people's growing disillusionment with the United States.

As a major world metropolis, Tehran is regularly visited by American journalists, both free-lance and regular correspondents. However Iran is far enough from the center of news that no American journalists are stationed there permanently. Iranian stringers are employed by the major journals and news services, but despite the general competence of these men they can hardly be expected to alert their clients to stories that would lead to their

16. Cottam, *Nationalism in Iran,* p. 307.

own arrests. At the same time, most of the Nationalist leaders are at liberty and could be interviewed by an enterprising journalist. The first phase of the policy-independent probe incorporates this approach.

When a representative of the American press who is known to be highly responsible calls on the Embassy, as he certainly would, a political officer should be designated to give him a rather special briefing. He should be given a factually accurate account of the Nationalist opposition, its leaders, factions, policies, and attitudes. The reporter should be told which of the Nationalists could be interviewed and how they could be reached. The point should be stressed that the reporter must at no time mention this briefing or the suggestion that he make contact with the Nationalist leaders. Also the reporter should be fully briefed on leading governmental personalities and advised to see as many of them as possible. The optimum results to be hoped for would be an article that was balanced and yet skeptical of a policy of 100 per cent support for the Shah. Since the Shah and many of his leading lieutenants are impressive and persuasive men, the journalist would see that the positive program of the government and governmental accomplishments are a far cry from the bleak picture painted for him by the Nationalists. On the other hand he would also understand that sincerely liberal men who are implacably opposed to communism are also violently hostile to the government and that even the best of programs is likely to fail unless it attracts the support of this element.

Very possibly, of course, the article when it appeared might lack the hoped-for balance. If so, reactions to the article would be of interest but no follow-up probing would be advisable. If the article approached the optimum, however, the next two or three weeks should be given to monitoring reactions. Such an article would be most unlikely to result in any action by the Iranian government, but if the journal involved were at all significant a revealing reaction could be expected. Since American support is regarded by the government and opposition as critical for the regime, any suggestion of a weakening of the American commitment is carefully studied. This article, which could easily pass unnoticed by the American public, would certainly be studied carefully in Iran. Iran's press is controlled and Iranians are given to projecting the image of their own press onto the foreign press. Therefore, it is likely that official American involvement will be suspected,[17] but enough is known of the American press for there to be no more than a suspicion.

Most closely to be observed would be the official reaction. Certainly no move should be made to elicit the government's reaction. If American diplomats should be questioned directly about it, their response should be to attest to the competence of the journalist but also to assert a lack of official American responsibility for what he writes. The temptation to disagree with the article should be resisted. The object would be to encourage an element of doubt regarding official involvement.

Reactions of National Front leaders could be easily monitored. A substantial exile press exists which could be expected to note and react to the article. Within Iran the reaction of National Front leaders could easily be ascertained indirectly even if the Embassy has no direct contacts. Rightist opposition elements will be in direct contact with the Embassy and no probing is likely to be necessary to explore their reactions. Soviet reactions, if any, could be noted in the reports of the two clandestine radio stations that broadcast into Iran. Any reaction other than a failure to take note of the article could tell a great deal.

This preliminary probe is, of course, a very mild one, but it is necessary to begin at this level to ascertain that there is in fact an

---

17. Sam Pope Brewer, "Unrest is Viewed as a Threat to Iran," *The New York Times,* January 2, 1958, p. 5. In reaction to this article the Shah called for a curtailment of activities of foreigners accused of interfering in Iran's internal affairs (*ibid.,* February 25, 1958, p. 2).

area of maneuverability with both the Shah and the noncommunist opposition. Assuming that the results conformed to expectations of a mild reaction, the second phase of the probe could be inaugurated to explore this area of maneuverability.

The second phase could take advantage of the separation of powers in the United States. In this action a junior Democratic senator who had criticized the governmental policy of supporting right-wing dictatorships could be utilized. He could be informed by a State Department representative that the government would not only not resent his airing his views but would even welcome a public statement by him evaluating our support of the Shah's regime. There is no reason whatsoever for the senator to say anything he did not believe. The optimum hope would be for the senator to accept the necessity of working with the Shah but to argue that unless the Shah engages in basic political reform any support of his regime would be useless. This is a much stronger probe and reactions from official and nonofficial groups could be anticipated.

The response to official formal and informal inquiries regarding the senator's statement should be similar to that described above. The point should be made that a United States senator even of the administration party is not an administration spokesman. But insofar as his views have any currency within Congress and the attentive public his attitude may be reflected in congressional appropriations. His remarks therefore should not be ignored, but neither should they be construed as representing a change in American policy. No effort should be made at this point to elicit information concerning official reactions to this speech, but unsolicited reactions from government officials and from the controlled press should be carefully analyzed.

No special effort should be necessary to gauge the response of National Front elements. The student and exile press published in the United States and Europe should tell a good deal about the continuing strength of the strategic objective of altering American foreign policy. It should also give some indication as to the characteristics of the leaders of the exile and student groups. An enthusiastic response to the statement would suggest that moderate leadership continues to prevail and that the Tudeh have as yet been unsuccessful in their efforts to gain a popular front. Similarly reactions of National Front leaders of various factional affiliations in Iran could lead to similar tentative answers.

During this phase of the probe, as with the first, the task of the American diplomatic community concerned with Iran would be primarily one of monitoring reactions. If an Iranian required a direct response from an American about the statement, the American should remind the questioner of the separation of powers in the United States, although some favorable asides regarding the competence and sincerity of the senator also would be in order. Other than the relevant official groups and the National Front, the group reactions of greatest interest would be the religious and right opposition, and the British, Soviet, and Middle East diplomats.

The third and final phase of the policy-independent probe would involve diplomatic conversation. This third phase, of course, would be inaugurated only if the earlier two phases had produced evidence pointing to the expected answers to the questions being probed. Assuming this is the case, a demonstration of official interest could be risked. The American diplomatic community could now go from monitoring to eliciting reactions to both the journal article and the senator's speech. This show of interest naturally would constitute a much stronger probing operation than either the article or the speech.

Since this phase is still in the policy-independent category, the task of eliciting information would be restricted to junior members of the diplomatic corps. Eliciting the views of the Shah and leading Iranian officials by highly placed American diplomats could very quickly take this probe into the policy-dependent category. An Iranian response necessitating an immediate American policy decision would be very possible. Eliciting views from Iranian officials should be done naturally and casually by junior American officers in conversations with second-level Iranian officials and pro-government politicians. The cocktail party or official reception would be the preferred locus for such conversations.

Eliciting the views of the National Front, religious opposition leaders, and leaders of the right-wing opposition need not be done so cautiously. The primary problem would be to make contact with members of these groups. Certainly a determined effort to reach these people merely to elicit responses to the senator's speech would be unwise. Iran is as yet an authoritarian and not a totalitarian state, however, and there are still some unique manifestations of the recent traditional order in society. Opposition leaders will very likely have spent some time in jail, their movements will probably be under surveillance, and their political activities will have been outlawed. But these leaders will in a surprising number of cases be relatives or friends of government officials and pro-government politicians. Therefore, the American diplomat in the normal course of his social activities will have natural contact with members of these groups, which makes possible a rather thorough exploration of the various opposition groups. Since each opposition group is certain to view American help as essential to the reversal of the group's fortunes, members of these groups are likely to be effusive in response to a remark concerning the senator's speech. Furthermore they will almost certainly know of the speech. Even though Iranian newspapers may make no reference to it, the *New York Times* has a broad enough circulation in Iran that any matter relating to Iranian politics is quickly known to the entire attentive public. This would be true also of the government-inspired article described in the first phase. Even if it were kept out of Iran, underground communications are good enough that translated copies would be in many hands very quickly. Therefore if a significant number of opposition leaders are queried a reasonably accurate response can be obtained.

If this show of interest did not produce a strongly adverse reaction anywhere, another procedure could be followed, which, at least in degree, is probably unique to states such as Iran where the tolerance range of interference is so broad. This involves the use of Iranians who are regarded as "close to the Americans." Far from resenting this image, many such individuals cultivate it and use it as a means for adding to their wealth and prestige. Since American economic and political influence are regarded as great, those who have access to the American ear are thought capable of helping an aspiring politician or business leader. But maintaining this image is not easy and the individual seeking to do so must demonstrate both access and influence on a continuing basis. If one or more of these men were asked by a junior diplomat, again casually, what the government and National Front reactions to the speech were, the officer could be fairly confident that within a matter of hours both government officials and National Front leaders would hear of the American interest. Reactions transmitted back to the Americans through this channel would be the reactions that government and National Front leaders would want the Americans to think they had had. The differential between these sets of reactions and those gained elsewhere could be very revealing.

The policy-independent probe could not be carried much beyond this point. Disavowal would still be possible but the pattern would be strong enough that credibility for the disavowal would not be great. For the purposes of the ideal foreign policy the assumption is made that the answers received from this probe correspond generally to expectations based on the situational analysis.

Tactical Planning: Phased Programming

After it is determined that there is indeed a significant area of maneuverability, the tactical planning necessary for the achievement of the strategic objectives can be undertaken. The basic strategic target is the dangerous polarization of the noncommunist Iranian attentive public. In order that trends working for the creation of a

broad noncommunist consensus can be set into motion or strengthened, the following tactical objectives should be achieved:

1) the accommodation of the Shah and the National Front with
the eventual acceptance by the Shah of a role as constitutional
monarch,

2) a gradual acceptance by the more moderate and constructive-
minded National Front leaders of positions in the government,

3) a commitment of the Nationalist opposition generally to a
constructive economic and social program that would retain the
essence of the third five-year plan,

4) the maintenance in positions of responsibility of those highly
trained and competent bureaucrats and army officers and their
acceptance as a part of a loyal bureaucracy by the Nationalists,

5) the continuance of an oil agreement compatible with Iranian
insistence on independence and an uninterrupted flow of revenue
from oil production, and

6) the continued membership of Iran in a CENTO which is far
more concerned with regional economic development than with an
increasingly irrelevant regional military strategy.

As described in the previous chapter, the first phase of tactical
planning must be prepared in careful detail. The central concern
must be to prepare a tactical scheme for the achievement of the
strategic objectives. This scheme, however, must include explicit
provisions for continual probing of the questions listed above. Even
if the policy-independent probing yielded returns that seemed to
confirm the situational analysis, the tactician must continue to regard the situational analysis as tentative. Before a tactical program
is initiated, therefore, a number of contingent plans should be
drawn up to which those executing the policy could turn if the
policy-connected probing were to demonstrate basic errors in the
situational analysis.

In the optimum tactical plan the first step must be a direct approach to the British. By the time the policy-independent probing has been completed, a good picture of British attitudes should have been gained. Iran's survival as an independent state has been dependent in no small part on the ability of Iranian statesmen to play off the great powers against each other. British opposition to the American strategic plan could easily be fatal, and therefore it is essential to try to secure British support or, at the very least, neutrality. The approach now could be a direct one.

Assuming a favorable British response a possible first stage optimum tactical plan could be as follows:

1) The American and British ambassadors should jointly or separately present a démarche to the Shah. This démarche should be prefaced by a statement indicating the continued support of the regime by both governments and giving assurance that their subsequent remarks are those of close allies and friends. The Shah should be informed, however, that the two governments have come to the conclusion that the widespread nature of opposition to the regime makes doubtful its ability to survive a really major crisis. The Iranian government's economic and social programs, the administrative reforms, and the land reform program, admirable though they are, are not really capable of providing in the near future the necessary broad support for the regime. The ambassadors further should state the conclusion of their governments that the inability of the court and the Nationalists to engage in fruitful negotiations has led them to presume to offer their good offices. Although a formal compromise is probably impossible to arrive at, the two governments believe a *modus vivendi* agreement is possible and would like to suggest the following proposals:

a. The Shah should permit them to inform opposition leaders that His Imperial Majesty is prepared to consider allowing the next parliamentary election to be free in the two Nationalist strongholds of Tehran and Tabriz and also in Kashan, the home of the moderate Iran Party leader, Allahyar Saleh. This will be done, however, only if the Nationalists are able to prepare a single election slate in each of these cities. The Shah should be reminded that although in all probability the delegations from these cities would be solidly Nationalist, the Majlis would remain overwhelmingly pro-government.

b. The Shah should permit the National Front to be offered the right to print a daily newspaper if it agrees not to attack the court, the security forces, the oil agreement, and CENTO, and if it agrees to follow a constructive line. Government censorship should be sufficient to enforce the provisions of this agreement.

c. The Shah should permit the advising of the National Front leaders that, if they are agreeable, several of their leading supporters with the requisite competence would be appointed to various subministerial posts.

The ambassadors should inform the Shah that their governments believe the sizeable Iranian middle class is really the Shah's natural ally in his desire to construct a stable and progressive regime. At present, however, the leadership of much of this class is bitter, disillusioned, or, if not intransigently hostile, apathetic. Thus the very element that should be the bulwark of the regime is the basis of its greatest vulnerability. The Shah further should be told of the conclusion that the Nationalists are becoming restive with their moderate leaders and are likely to turn to men advocating direct action, including terror. Should such men dominate the movement, Iran's vulnerability to communism will be increased.

2) Simultaneously the National Front should be advised officially of the proposals made to the Shah. Carrying out this task would be one of the most difficult aspects of the assignment. Since the National Front is faction-ridden and since a basic objective would be to reverse the trend toward extremist leadership, the greatest care must be taken to avoid giving the impression of favoring one or another faction. In presenting these proposals to National Front representatives the ambassadors should stress the point that this approach does not constitute in any way a withdrawal of support

from the Shah. Rather it reflects the conclusions of the two governments that the western powers, the Shah, and the National Front all have the same general objectives for Iran, i.e., the growth of a strong, stable, and independent government. The two governments believe that the differences of the Shah and the National Front are reconcilable but they realize that more than words are necessary to prove this point. Therefore this program is being presented to grant the opportunity for the two sides to demonstrate their good will.

These additional points should be made to the National Front regarding the program outlined to the Shah:

a. The representatives of the various Nationalist factions should be advised that the two governments regard the formation of a single election slate as an absolute prerequisite to the success of the program. Since any faction not participating would be granted a major demagogic advantage in being able to depict the other factions as having sold out to western imperialism, a failure to establish a single slate would nullify the agreement. The two governments should also stress the point that the men selected for these slates would be placed in a position as spokesmen for the Nationalist movement. They should therefore include experienced and responsible leaders since the image they project will in large part determine the success or failure of this program.

b. Regarding the newspaper, a similar point should be made. Although the Shah could hardly be expected to withdraw censorship immediately, there will be a wide area of freedom to present alternative programs and to criticize official corruption and incompetence. Again the success or failure of the program depends on the editorial staff and editorial policy of the paper. If restraint is shown and an emphasis is placed on constructive criticism and alternative positive programs, the probability exists that the scope of freedom of the paper would be steadily expanded.

3) Also simultaneously the entire American and British official

communities should in their contacts with Iranians advance the argument for accommodation. Any sign of disagreement or lack of enthusiasm within either community could be seized upon by a reluctant Shah as affording an opportunity for smashing an unwanted program. Religious leaders in particular should be sought out and told of the efforts being made to increase the freedom of activity within the country. Members of the rightist opposition should in no way be encouraged to believe that western sponsorship would be granted them.

This program is designed to continue probing in the policy-independent stage and simultaneously to set into motion the desired trend alteration. If the Shah proved to be amenable to the program, this would serve as strongly affirmative answers to the first and second questions concerning his responsiveness to pressure and his willingness to move toward a more constitutional role. If the various Nationalist factional leaders were able to agree to the program, their agreement would provide persuasive answers to questions three through seven. All of this would indicate that the Nationalists were willing to cooperate with the West, that moderate leadership still prevails, that Tudeh efforts to form a popular front have been unsuccessful, and that the Nationalists were indeed capable of accepting the Shah in a constitutional monarch role. The other questions would begin receiving tentative answers as the program was put into effect.

The first phase of the tactical scheme, if successful, should begin to alter the trends in the first two strategic levels described above. The first level referred to an increasing conviction that the West's commitment to an authoritarian royalist regime was total and that there was a decreasing interest among the Nationalists in altering American foreign policy toward Iran. This program should produce the desired alteration of these trends. The second strategic level was concerned with altering the polarization trends of the community. Here too the program, if accepted, should set into motion the desired trend alterations leading to a move by the Shah toward constitutionalism and an acceptance of this altered regime by the Nationalists.

As soon as the program has been advanced and its existence has become known, a monitoring of bureaucratic and army officer reactions must begin. Almost inevitably members of the professional core of the bureaucracy and army officers will begin to wonder if they have not made a mistake in granting an implicit association with the regime. If the ideal gradualistic program actually goes into effect, the Nationalists should begin to accept this professional core as above partisan conflict and therefore an asset for the Nationalist constructive program. But if morale deteriorates too rapidly a move to one of the contingency tactical schemes would seem to be in order.

Unfavorable answers to the questions regarding the responses of the Soviet Union, China, Turkey, and the Arab states are most unlikely at this early tactical stage. The Arab states generally, with the exceptions of Jordan, Tunisia, Morocco, and Saudi Arabia, have called for an alteration of the Iranian regime in this direction. The Soviet Union, too, would be most unlikely to consider altering its strategy, although charges that the Nationalists had entered into a conspiracy with western imperialism could be expected. Turkey could react adversely and if Premier Menderes were still in power it probably would. However, sentiment in the Turkish armed forces and among Turkish intellectuals for a less total indentification with the West is appearing. Many Turks would therefore welcome these changes and an adverse official response might in fact add to American power in dealing with Turkey. At a later tactical stage modifications might be necessary as these foreign reactions are assessed.

If the answers to the questions were favorable and if evidence appeared that the desired trend alterations are developing, the second tactical phase of the optimum tactical scheme could be put into effect. This should not imply that the first tactical phase would result in the creation of a new static plateau. Were a Nationalist newspaper authorized, the editors would surely be exploring their bounds of freedom of reporting and seeking to broaden these bounds. Those Nationalists occupying subministerial posts would be attempting to broaden their policy role. And aspiring Nationalist politicians in cities other than Tabriz, Tehran, and Kashan would be maneuvering for the day when elections in their areas too would be free. Hopefully there would also be an increasing though implicit acceptance of professionals in the bureaucracy and army. The optimum second-phase tactical scheme in fact would be simply one of steadily relaxing controls over opposition political activity.

Contingent second-phase tactical schemes would be devised for each of the major possible answers that might diverge sharply from those expected. For instance, an immediate tactical retreat would be required by unfavorable answers regarding the Shah's willingness to agree to an implicit rapprochement with the Nationalists and to his willingness to accept a reduction in his influence. Had the policy-independent probes been carried out carefully enough, indications of a possible drastic response should have been seen. The unfavorable answers therefore would more likely be manifestations of a serious reconsideration of his own strategy by the Shah. These would probably be seen in one of three directions: the possibility of abdication, the advisability of a severe crackdown on Nationalist politicians, or an exploring of the likely consequences of a swing toward neutrality. American power is weak enough that a show of serious interest in any of these alternatives could compel a tactical reversal and even a strategic reversal. For example, if it should become apparent that not only would the Shah reject this program but that he would respond by arresting once again all the leading Nationalist politicians, the United States would be virtually unable to give support to these men. Only by threatening to alter the type of relationship could the United States gain the needed leverage strength, and this threat, to be credible, must reflect a serious re-consideration of basic American strategy in the Middle East.

If a continuance of the basic strategy is assumed, a new tactical scheme would have to be devised for striking at the problem presented by the sharp political polarization in Iran. One possibility would be to begin a series of policy-independent probes to discover the existence within the bureaucracy or security forces of men who understood the need for attracting increased support for the regime from the middle-class and religious leadership and who were capable of executing programs for this purpose. What this calls for is an effort to achieve the strategic objective through tactical schemes that proceed at a much slower pace than the optimal.

A second major area that might produce unfavorable answers would be that concerning the moderate leadership of the Nationalists, the progress of the Tudeh in seeking support for a popular front, and the willingness of the Nationalists to agree to the Shah's remaining as a constitutional leader. Were the program offered by American and British representatives rejected, the supposition could be drawn that unfavorable answers to at least one of these questions had been received. Since the number of Nationalists being contacted would be large, there would be an excellent chance that the reason or reasons for rejection would be learned. Furthermore, if the policy-independent probes had not led to an expectation of this rejection, there would be a good supposition, which also could probably be confirmed, that the Nationalists were deeply divided on this matter. Here again a tactical retreat would be in order and new policy-independent probing would be called for. The most likely alternative tactical scheme now to be advanced would be one that would seek to attract moderate-led factions into a program similar to that described in the first tactical phase, while at the same time continuing to suppress the communications and activity of the extremist-led or Tudeh-influenced factions.

A third major area in which unfavorable answers could be received is that of the morale of the members of the bureaucracy and security forces. The professional-minded officers are particularly vulnerable here. In many cases they will have come from middle-class families, many of whose members are bitterly antiregime. Consequently there is likely to be a good deal of ambivalence regarding the regime and more than a suspicion that their having sided with the regime will destroy their future in a successor regime if one should materialize. Therefore the inauguration of a program that has as a clear end the inclusion of Nationalist leaders in a government could set off a reaction of panic. SAVAK officers would have serious reason to recall the treatment of their counterparts in Iraq, Hungary, and Cuba when unpopular dictatorial regimes were toppled. Should morale break down, there would be a serious possibility that a gradual liberalization program could become a revolution.

The contingent response called for might be no more than a slowdown of the optimum tactical plan. Were the situation to appear more serious, however, a major tactical retreat would be necessary, calling for an exploration of the kinds of assurances that would be necessary for the professionals and of the speed with which replacement of vulnerable officers with less vulnerable ones could be undertaken.

The fact should be noted that if the optimum tactical scheme were to prove generally successful in achieving the strategic objectives the United States–Iranian leverage system would be automatically and significantly altered. The new system would resemble more that of the United States and India as described in Chapter Two. The Iranian range of tolerance for interference would narrow as consensus regarding the government increased and the lever that granted the United States much of its power, i.e., the perceived vulnerability to exploitation of domestic political dissatisfaction, would lose most of its strength. Subsequent tactical schemes therefore would have to reflect these basic changes.

The strategic objectives of current American policy toward Iran are clear enough. They are to maintain the regime in power while over the long run attempting to establish a broad consensus for the regime based on programs of economic and social reform. Administration improvements, sensible economic planning, and land reform programs are the goals the American government apparently wishes the Iranian government to pursue. There is no available evidence indicating that political reforms designed to attract the eventual support of the politically active and generally hostile middle-class, intellectual, and religious elements are regarded as important. Maintaining Iran in the western camp may be slightly declining in importance but nevertheless it is still signficant.

Based on a comparison of the ideal and actual policies of the United States toward Iran the following conclusion is suggested:

The American government is in fact concerned with the long run in its policy toward Iran. The trends that it seeks to strengthen are those adding to Iran's productivity, economic stability, and administrative efficiency. These trends are apparently the ones assumed to be critical in the establishment of long-term stability in Iran. There is no evidence indicating a direct concern with political polarization or even a very serious awareness of it. Certainly no external evidence exists of efforts to persuade the Iranian government to make peace with its noncommunist and largely middle-class opposition. Implicitly accepted is an economic determinism, which assumes that political stability results if economic and land reform programs are adopted. No evidence whatsoever exists indicating any dismay on the part of the American government with the totalitarian drift so long as that drift is in the direction of an all-powerful structure in the administrative state order. The fact, if it is accepted as a fact, that much of the intelligentsia, including many individuals who are American-trained, are alienated is presumably dismissed as a temporary malaise. There is an implicit doctrinaireness, but it is a doctrine much closer to W. W. Rostow's noncommunist manifesto[18] than to a concern for liberal democracy. However, the conclusion is worth considering that the doctrinaire aspect and in fact the long-term focus is less the consequence of following a rigid recipe of questionable validity than a culmination of ad hoc responses. The only area in which American support was welcomed by the regime in the past was in economic and administrative reform. After several years of attacking specific problems, American officials in Iran gradually realized that, partly because of their programs but mostly because of oil revenue, trends toward economic growth and administrative reform were taking shape. These trends seemed to these officials to be consonant with the general American strategic objective, as indeed they are also in the ideal policy, and were therefore to be encouraged.

If the above explanation is valid, the long-term focus that exists is less the result of Mr. Rostow's influence than it is the result of circumstances. A comparison with the ideal policy indicates that the American government does not make the kind of situational analysis called for in the ideal type policy and has little understanding of capability in terms of leverage. Since the intimate American involvement in the overthrow of Dr. Mossadeq in August, 1953, American policy, at least as overtly recorded, manifests little concern with political engineering. Instead there has been a long series of decisions to strengthen the post-Mossadeq regimes through budgetary, general economic, technical, and military assistance. What little pressure has been applied has been in the direction of economic and administrative efficiency. Political engineering therefore falls into the crisis syndrome. Gross interference is resorted to, as in 1953, which upsets the entire evolutionary pattern of Iranian political development. The United States then withdraws from direct political concern and almost totally disregards responsibility for postrevolutionary political developments. The government re-

18. W. W. Rostow, *The Stages of Economic Growth* (Cambridge, Mass., 1960).

treats to dealing indirectly with political problems through programs of economic and military assistance. There is nothing to indicate a direct concern with the attitudinal base of political polarization or anti-American sentiments by either the American government or press. Instead there persists a simple faith in the eventual success of an economic reform program in achieving control through attitudinal consensus. Presumably if polarization should lead to overt political rebellion, American interference will once again be at the most audacious level, as in Guatemala, Lebanon, the Dominican Republic, and South Vietnam, or defeat will be accepted as in Iraq, depending on an instantaneous assessment of capability. The proposition that the crisis itself could be avoided by political trend manipulation has not been confronted.

It follows that capability in terms of leverage is little understood. American ambassadors since 1953 have sought conscientiously to create an impression of total commitment to the regime. In fact they have consistently made the point that the survival of the regime is a matter of vital American strategic concern. They appear to assume, somehow, that easy and smooth personal relations are the vital ingredient of influence rather than a strong situational bargaining position. Having divested themselves of the power to pressure the regime into making the necessary effort to reduce polarization and to attract increasing support, the Americans involved seem to have ignored this possibility and accepted the immense risk that assassination presents to the stability of that highly polarized community. The result is a continuance of elite structure, value, perceptual, and attitudinal trends that are working against the achievement of the clear American strategic objectives of a stable, noncommunist Iran.

5 THE INSTITUTIONAL BASE FOR AMERICAN DIPLOMACY

THE COMPARISON in the previous chapter of an ideal American foreign policy toward Iran with actual policy suggested that postwar American diplomacy remains essentially ad hoc in style. Despite the expansion of the American foreign policy community and a vastly improved communications system, policy is still very much a series of responses to specific challenges. The comparison further suggests the basic reason for the continuance of this style of diplomacy. A foreign policy concerned with the long range must focus, whether implicitly or explicitly, on the alteration or reinforcement of relevant political, economic, and social trends. And plans for trend alteration must be based on situational analyses in which the relevant trends are identified and carefully examined. In some respects the institutional response of American diplomacy to the problems of the nuclear age has been impressive, but thus far the institutional base for constructing the necessary situational analyses has not been developed. It is the purpose of this chapter to look at the expanded American foreign policy institutional base and to suggest one means by which it might be improved.

Very shortly after World War II the Truman administration sensed that the scope of diplomatic activity must be broadened substantially and in several directions. With the inauguration of the Point IV program a beginning was made toward constructing an institutional base for planning and executing programs to manipulate economic and social trends and, indirectly, political trends in certain target states. The United States Information Agency represented the institutionalization of efforts to manipulate politically relevant trends in attitudes. And the creation of the Central Intelligence Agency marked an acceptance of the need to provide an institutional base for manipulating certain political and attitudinal trends by covert means. In each case the new institution was created in response to a series of clearly perceived specific challenges. But in sum they added up to a substantial, multilevel base for dealing with perceived foreign policy problems.

Unfortunately there has not been a parallel comprehension of the opportunity afforded by this elaborate institutional base for a co-ordinated, broad-scoped diplomacy. In each case the newly created agency has been granted considerable autonomy and has engaged in an effort to discover some inner logic for its institutional role. Still, in spite of this and a very considerable confusion regarding their roles, there has been a drift toward institutional integration especially at the working level. These points can be illustrated by a brief look at the Central Intelligence Agency and the serious confusion that surrounds the problem of dealing with covert diplomacy.

THE C.I.A. AND DIPLOMACY

Andrew Tully, the author of a heavily romanticized account of the Central Intelligence Agency, states that the Bay of Pigs failure, devastating though it was, may in the long run prove to have been a good thing.[1] This judgment is based on the assumption that the re-evaluation of the C.I.A.'s role in the formulation and execution of foreign policy that followed the Cuban fiasco resulted in a substantial narrowing of the scope of the C.I.A.'s activities. Since the

1. Andrew Tully, *CIA: The Inside Story* (New York, 1962), p. 267.

re-evaluation that took place will not be made public, Tully's assumption cannot be verified, but the appointment a few months later of John A. McCone as Director of Central Intelligence argues strongly that the C.I.A.'s role was indeed being restricted. Were the Kennedy administration planning to continue granting the agency a major voice in foreign policy determination as was done during Allen Dulles' tenancy, the man chosen to replace Dulles would surely have had a broad background in and sophisticated understanding of foreign affairs. The selection of a man whose reputation was that of an exceptional administrator with a great deal of experience in the security community but with little exposure to the intricacies of international politics indicates a sharply altered view of the purpose and function of the C.I.A. and its director.

Presumably the Kennedy administration wanted as the Director of Central Intelligence (D.C.I.) someone who could seize control of, tighten, and rationalize the administrative structure of the C.I.A. and who could improve considerably its functional integration in the security community. Also presumably Kennedy did not want anyone whose primary interests would include the substance of foreign policy. A lack of experience in intelligence collecting and collating is no handicap. That is a highly technical skill, and as long as the D.C.I. ensures that every important target is well covered and that the intelligence product is frequently and expertly tested, he will be performing adequately.

The McCone appointment is good evidence that the Kennedy administration drew from the Cuban experience the conclusion that the C.I.A. was delving too much in diplomatic and military fields. If Tully's and other's accounts of its activities in the Cuban operation are even close to the truth, this conclusion and the drastic reduction in the C.I.A.'s role are understandable.[2] The near in-

2. *Ibid.;* Paul W. Blackstock, *The Strategy of Subversion* (Chicago, 1964); Tad Szulc and Karl E. Meyer, *The Cuban Invasion: The Chronicle of a Disaster* (New York, 1962); David Wise and Thomas Ross, *The Invisible Government* (New York, 1964).

subordination involved and the indifference to the damage done to the international image of the United States would alone call for a thorough re-evaluation.

But the contention here is that a different conclusion should have been drawn from the Bay of Pigs. The Cuban failure points instead to the lack of institutional integration and to the lack of a theoretical base for a strategy designed to meet the demands of one major aspect of the Cold War challenge: the internal threat of communism in much of Asia, Africa, and Latin America.

THE C.I.A. AND NONATTRIBUTABILITY

Possibly the one aspect of the Cuban operation that now, after the event, seems the most unreal is the apparent belief that responsibility for an operation of this magnitude would not be attributed to the United States government by governments and peoples throughout the world. Yet available evidence argues that those doing the planning did not anticipate such attribution.[3] This failure to anticipate the United States' being held responsible provides a key for understanding some of the elements in the confusion surrounding the C.I.A.'s foreign policy role generally.

The partisan attacks that were directed against the administration for the Bay of Pigs failure carried an immutable logic and can be summarized as follows: It is understandable considering the intense suspicion of the United States in Latin America that an American government would avoid scrupulously any crude and easily attributable interference in Latin American affairs. However, having decided that Castro must be toppled by an openly American-backed Cuban revolutionary force, the United States had everything to gain and nothing further to lose by making certain that this

3. Haynes Johnson, *The Bay of Pigs: The Leaders' Story of Brigade 2506* (New York, 1964), pp. 66–67; Arthur Schlesinger, Jr., *A Thousand Days: John F. Kennedy in the White House* (Cambridge, Mass., 1965), especially pp. 242–43.

attack would succeed. To accept all of the opprobrium of crude interference and then to add to it the additional indignity of defeat at the hands of a minor if particularly obnoxious tyrant is unforgivable. The administration tickled every anti-American funny bone in Latin America and simultaneously reinforced the belief in Yankee imperialism.

To have answered these partisan critics with the statement that the United States did not expect the world to blame us would have been to appear hopelessly naïve. Kennedy as a candidate for the presidency had made clear his intentions to aid the anti-Castro forces. Quite obviously in April, 1961, he expected the world to understand that we had given material support to the rebels. But at some fine point the line was drawn which in the administration's mind separated intervention from legitimate sympathetic support. Two aspects of the behavior of the administration at this time illustrate the failure to anticipate world reaction. According to several accounts, Adlai Stevenson was not told of the extent of our involvement until the operation was about to begin,[4] and Kennedy announced less than a week before the invasion that United States forces would never be involved in Cuba. Had they expected that the invasion would be attributed to the United States, Stevenson would surely have been carefully prepared for the difficult diplomatic task of explaining our actions in the United Nations, and Kennedy would certainly not have made a statement that in retrospect appears to be utterly cynical.

The explanation generally given for the Cuban failure is that American intelligence was seriously faulty and circumstances argue the validity of this charge. But this is only one part and a long way from being the major part of the total explanation. In seeking a

4. Johnson, *The Bay of Pigs,* p. 92; Szulc and Meyer, *The Cuban Invasion,* p. 110; Wise and Ross, *The Invisible Government,* pp. 15–17; Blackstock, *The Strategy of Subversion,* p. 247; Tully, *CIA,* pp. 252–53; Schlesinger, *A Thousand Days,* p. 271.

more fundamental aspect of this explanation it might be well to ask why official Washington could be led to expect nonattributability. A major clue here is to be found in the somewhat undeserved aura of success which at that time surrounded the C.I.A. in Washington. It is now accepted by much of the informed American public that the Arbenz government in Guatemala and the Mossadeq government in Iran were earlier and more successful targets of major C.I.A. operations.[5] In both cases the effort involved seems to have been minimal and in both cases plans apparently called for nonattributability. However, the evidence in these cases suggests that the element of good luck was extraordinarily important. This is particularly true in the case of Iran, where the original coup attempt failed and the Shah fled in undignified haste. Mossadeq's overthrow three days later was more due to the excesses of the communist Tudeh Party, which appalled much of the urban Iranian population by its behavior and confirmed many of the previously doubted claims that Iran was on the verge of a communist take-over.[6] In Guatemala sufficiently significant defections occurred within the security forces to give victory to a movement which could not have gained that victory without such defections. Furthermore the well-informed in the Middle East and Latin America have from the very first attributed these overthrows to the United States.[7] The expectations of nonattributability were fulfilled only in the United States, where even the informed American public was generally oblivious for many months and even years to this new image the United States government was acquiring abroad.

The Cuban affair was in effect the legacy of the Iranian and Guatemalan successes. Both of these adventures seem to indicate

5. Richard and Gladys Harkness, "Mysterious Doings of the CIA," *Saturday Evening Post,* November 6, 1954, pp. 34–35.

6. Richard W. Cottam, *Nationalism in Iran* (Pittsburgh, Pa., 1964), pp. 225–26.

7. *Ibid.,* p. 227; *The New York Times,* June 24, 1954, p. 3.

inadequate preparation and a refusal to confront seriously the implications of attributability. But security requirements were so interpreted as to prevent any but the highest level administration officials from being made aware of these operations. Consequently the men who made the final decisions and who assessed the results were men who, regardless of competence, could not have had the detailed understanding of Iranian or Guatemalan affairs to make an intelligent judgment of the adequacy of the plans or to evaluate the contention of nonattributability. By the time the Cuban case came under discussion, the C.I.A.'s past successes must have argued very strongly in favor of the operation and the expectations of nonattributability. They should have argued the opposite. The failure to recognize inadequate planning, and the inability to understand that nonattributability was impossible for an operation of this magnitude, should be seen as symptomatic of the larger failure to comprehend the diplomatic role of the C.I.A. and to provide a rational institutionalization of that role. This failure is the real father of the Cuban fiasco.

THE C.I.A. AND FOREIGN POLICY FORMULATION

One of the most unfortunate consequences of the Cuban misadventure has been the alteration of the C.I.A.'s popular image. Tully's book, along with *The U-2 Affair* and *The Invisible Government* by Thomas Ross and David Wise, *The Bay of Pigs* by Haynes Johnson, and Fred Cook's study add up to at best a picture of romantic juvenility. Going beyond this, Cook adds the element of insensitivity to liberal values and the suspicion of right-wing extremism.[8] There is little question but that in liberal circles at least there is now a deep suspicion of the C.I.A. and a desire to see that organization tightly fettered. The C.I.A. probably did in fact

8. Fred Cook, "CIA," *The Nation*, June 24, 1961, p. 570. Cook refers to C.I.A. as a "comintern in right wing robes."

merit criticism and a serious overhaul may have been in order. But a reaction against it resulting in the removal of that organization from direct participation in the formulation and execution of American foreign policy would have been a move in the wrong direction.

Two basic prescriptive implications of this study are that the American diplomatic style must be altered in two directions. First, strategy must be based on a thorough situational analysis rather than on the intuition of skilled diplomats. Second, the concept of diplomacy must be greatly expanded if the United States is to perform well in an era in which competitive interference is a primary aspect of the international struggle. Quite clearly the day in which diplomacy was little more than official negotiation, observation, and reporting has passed. The diplomacy now called for is a far more active one that must seek to strengthen, alter, or reverse short-range and long-range trends throughout the world, and some of this activity can be carried out only by covert means. Any expectation that the Department of State would undertake in the immediate post-World War II era the covert activities necessary for trend alteration was foredoomed. A deeply entrenched bureaucratic style of behavior cannot be revolutionized so quickly. But the problem was much too compelling to be ignored and an institutional approach to its solution made a good deal of sense. Lacking any paralyzing traditions and possessing an activist temperament, the C.I.A. was in many ways the ideal locus for many of the new activities that were called for. But the proviso must quickly be added that an institutional arrangement for a very close and careful integration of its diplomatic activities and those of the Department of State needed to have been made from the beginning.

The National Security Act of 1947 that brought the C.I.A. into existence was certainly not intended by its authors to grant it a policy-making function. Yet the phraseology of that act is ambiguous on this point and understandably so. An argument that the C.I.A. should be kept completely out of policy formulation makes sense only if the concept of policy-making is a very restricted one.

If the C.I.A. is to be effective in the more clandestine aspects of diplomacy it must be granted a good deal of freedom to interpret and to improvise upon stated general policy. Such interpretations and improvisations are in reality vital aspects of policy formulation. A C.I.A. officer intimately involved in important diplomatic maneuvers, if he is a man of any competence, ought to have proposals for further action that should be carefully studied by officers closer to the locus of high-level decision-making. All of this is obvious enough, yet the suspicion seems warranted that the stricture against policy-making by the C.I.A. has on occasion been interpreted so narrowly that the balancing effect of the perspective of the C.I.A. officer is frequently lost with the high-level decision-makers. At this level one of the prime essentials is that the perspectives of men in State, the C.I.A., and Defense be understood and balanced and that policy should integrate the activities of all three.

The C.I.A.'s clandestine diplomatic role received its statutory authorization in the phrase providing that it shall perform "other functions and duties" as directed by the National Security Council. But neither the authors of this statute nor those who subsequently reviewed the C.I.A.'s role clarified the inherent contradiction in assigning it a major diplomatic task without granting a consonant role in policy formulation. Given the United States' traditional diplomatic style and the deeply ingrained belief that interference per se is bad, excluding the C.I.A. from policy is understandable. Yet the hypothesis is worth some attention that the statutory exclusion of the C.I.A. from policy-making had the paradoxical result of turning policy over to the organization at critical moments.

Denying a formal policy-making role to the C.I.A. would, unhappily, not influence in any way the appearance of the kind of situations that have led to covert political activities. Such situations are a constant in this period of the world's history and the administration can avoid giving the C.I.A. major foreign policy tasks only if other agencies can properly execute them. For example, the suggestion was commonly made after the Cuban failure that the Department of Defense take over most of the C.I.A.'s paramilitary functions.[9] But such a step would surely have been a serious retrogression. The C.I.A.'s failure in Cuba was in part the result of an uncoordinated splintering of institutional responsibility and in part a failure in political sophistication. Paramilitary operations are in essence political operations with military overtones rather than the reverse. To grant priority to the military aspects and to do nothing fundamental about the lack of coordination in the foreign affairs community could not result in improvement but would almost certainly result in even less political sophistication. Similarly, those aspects of C.I.A. activities which could be characterized as covert diplomacy could be transferred to the Department of State. But the mode of operations in State has been such that giving that department this task would mean only that the task would be interpreted out of existence. There is the likelihood, therefore, that when such tasks as these can no longer be ignored the C.I.A. will be assigned to carry them out. And since no effective control mechanism has been devised for the Agency, the effect once again would be that of granting an occasional carte blanche to it.

CONTROL OF THE C.I.A.

The problem of controlling the C.I.A. has deeply concerned men within the executive branch of government, within the Congress, and within the attentive public. Such concern is only natural given the necessity that C.I.A. operations be concealed from all those without a compelling "need to know." The possibility that a small group of bureaucrats could in carrying out these operations involve

9. *The New York Times,* April 29, 1961, p. 1.

an unaware government and people in crises of a most serious nature is a haunting one. Yet the contention here is that a focus on formal control devices for the C.I.A. is essentially misdirected. Real control of the Agency can be accomplished only if (a) the type of covert diplomatic activity performed by it is fully recognized as one aspect of an integrated diplomatic strategy and (b) C.I.A. representatives have participated fully in drawing up the plans for an overall diplomatic strategy. Only by fully integrating the C.I.A. in the policy-making and -executing process can it be thought of as being controlled.

Of course, C.I.A. representatives have been included in government counsels at all levels and the D.C.I. has had ready access to the president. But such access does not result in a functional integration of the organization if the C.I.A. representatives are thought of and think of themselves as essentially supportive rather than policy-generating. The appointment by President Johnson of Admiral William F. Raborn to succeed John McCone as D.C.I. in 1965 argues that in the Johnson as in the Kennedy administration the view of the C.I.A. was that of a supportive but not policy generative agency. Admiral Raborn was if anything less well equipped and less inclined to play a role in foreign policy formulation than McCone had been.

However, there was a sharp reaction to the type of leadership that Admiral Raborn could be expected to and apparently did provide. His replacement in 1966 by Richard Helms, a career officer with broad experience in the foreign policy field, may herald a new era for the C.I.A.'s status in the foreign policy community. Presumably Helms has the experience and understanding of the organization's function in the diplomatic field to advance the integration of its role within a more broadly conceived diplomacy. Such an eventuality is all the more possible since even during the McCone and Raborn tenancies bureaucratic developments in Washington and in embassies abroad were pointing to advances in the integration of the C.I.A. on a working level into the foreign policy complex.

The key institution for integrating the agency in overseas activities is the "country team," which is presided over by the ambassador and is composed of the heads of the various United States government agencies in the host state. In theory and even more frequently in practice the ambassador not only coordinates but gives direction to all American activities in that state. President Kennedy assumed as did the Senate subcommittee headed by Senator Jackson that a genuine functional integration of American overseas activities necessitates the granting of strong powers to the ambassador in the country team.[10] In letters to the various ambassadors President Kennedy made this point very clear, but despite his directive the country team has been far from meeting expectations. The ambassador is an officer in the Foreign Service and the perspective of the Foreign Service will inevitably dominate his approach. More likely than not he will share the dislike of the C.I.A. that is widespread among his colleagues. Sensing this, C.I.A. officers might well continue to respond, as it is believed they have done in the past, by concealing much of what they do. Similar behavior could be expected from U.S.I.A., A.I.D., and the military missions abroad.

The answer here might well be to give teeth to the country team concept by giving the ambassador and the second-ranking diplomatic officer full and complete, rather than—as is now the case— *pro forma,* access to all files, requiring that all substantive communications to Washington pass through the hands of the ambassador and giving the ambassador veto right over any of these communications. But such a move will result in integration only if

10. For a published account of the Senate Subcommittee on National Security Staffing and Operations study see Henry M. Jackson, ed., *The Secretary of State and the Ambassador: Jackson Subcommittee Papers on the Conduct of American Foreign Policy* (New York, 1964).

the ambassador is held personally responsible for the proper functioning of the country team as a whole and of each of its components. And this should certainly include responsibility for covert diplomacy. An essential institutional provision should be a mechanism by which the career assessment of the ambassador would be based on an evaluation of his performance in each of the areas of responsibility, an evaluation made by a board consisting of representatives of each of the agencies involved. With his career advancement and future assignments dependent on his success in coordinating and directing all of the agencies involved, a marked change in perspective should follow. Similarly, in considering the career progress of the leading C.I.A., U.S.I.A., A.I.D., and military mission personnel, each agency should be under obligation to consider reports submitted by the ambassador regarding the individual performances on the country team. With such a strengthening of the country team concept, the possibility of the ambassador's being able to orchestrate the actions of the entire team would be considerably enhanced.

Similar advances have been made and are being made toward the functional integration of the C.I.A. in Washington. President Kennedy dropped the ineffective Operations Coordinating Board and substituted the task force concept. For each foreign policy problem area task forces were set up to study the situation and recommend governmental policy. Included in each task force were C.I.A. representatives who had a thorough understanding of the area and of the operational problem for executing covert diplomacy there. This allowed for an integration of the C.I.A. perspective at a working level. In 1966 a major step toward further institutional integration was taken with the setting up of interdepartmental committees. The easy acceptance of this innovation within the Department of State argues that a stylistic transformation has indeed occurred there. Truly effective execution of covert diplomacy and the control of this aspect of the C.I.A. requires the acceptance by the Department of State of the place of covert diplomacy in overall diplomatic activity and the willingness of the Department of State to assume full responsibility for the planning and conduct of covert diplomacy. If present trends continue, the day may not be far away in which these requisites will be fulfilled.

VIETNAM: A CASE OF DIPLOMATIC FAILURE?

Any assessment of American diplomatic performance in the mid-1960's must include a critique of the case of Vietnam. In this period the China littoral, and particularly Vietnam, was the most important arena of American diplomatic activity. A conclusion that the Vietnamese case represents a diplomatic failure therefore should not be lightly drawn. Yet there is a strong prima-facie case for such a judgment. It is a commonplace to observe that the Vietnamese struggle is essentially a political one and that the immediate political objective of American diplomacy has been the creation of a stable, noncommunist government in South Vietnam. And it is stating the obvious to note that the Saigon government in 1966 was farther from meeting this objective than was the Saigon government in 1963.

This conclusion of failure need not, of course, argue that the failure was either avoidable or is permanent. It may well be that the problem of developing a stable regime proved to be far greater than anticipated and that a near-colonial policy in which American troops virtually occupy the country, American advisors are found at all governmental levels, and American economic and technical aid is vast was necessary for the ultimate achievement of that objective. If such is the case, the sealing off of the border of South Vietnam at the 17th parallel and the pacification of the countryside south of that parallel were only logical prerequisites. No attempt will or could be made here to evaluate this point. Such an evaluation would call for an expert knowledge and a detailed understanding of American policy in the area, which this writer lacks.

However, overt American diplomatic behavior in the Vietnam area does support three basic observations. First, the American involvement in Vietnam has been the result of a series of ad hoc responses to perceived communist challenges to the authority of the Saigon government. There is no evidence to indicate that the kind of detailed and operationally relevant situational analysis of the Vietnam problem was made from which a long-term plan could be drawn. All of the concerned governmental agencies were brought into Vietnam and the commitment of each steadily increased, but the kind of unity that a long-range plan could produce was lacking.

Second, efforts to bring about a coalition of noncommunist forces in Vietnam have been sporadic and conducted at too high a level. Such behavior is understandable. As the Iranian case study indicates, approaching and negotiating with the opposition to a government dependent on American support for its continued existence is extraordinarily difficult. The easiest course in Vietnam as in Iran has been to give all-out support to the government in power. To simultaneously negotiate with the opposition and give the necessary support to the government calls for more than finesse; it calls for a thorough integration of the instrument of covert diplomacy and coordinated direction from the ambassador. It also calls for a tightly constructed target analysis of the political forces of Vietnam including the National Liberation Front.

Third, the necessary relating of United States policy in Vietnam to policy elsewhere has not been done. As was pointed out in Chapter Three, the impact of American policy in Vietnam on every other aspect of American foreign policy has been so great as to threaten a systemic change. Containment, a term which described the sum of a large number of American foreign policy actions, is ceasing to be descriptive of American policy. Furthermore, there is little to indicate that the impact of our Vietnam policy on internal political developments in the Soviet Union, China, western Europe, and the smaller states on the Chinese littoral was anticipated or is even recognized.

What these observations add up to is a conclusion that the type of diplomatic problem that today confronts various foreign offices requires elaborate, objective, and operationally relevant situational analyses; the orchestration of an institutional complex designed to deal with all aspects of the diplomatic problem; and a careful relating of specific planning to overall policy. Lacking this, policy is likely to continue as ad hoc responses to immediate challenges. The discussion of the confusion that has surrounded the diplomatic function of the C.I.A. has pointed to one direction in which an improvement of performance can be expected. That direction is the functional integration of all the agencies involved in the conduct of foreign policy; and indeed progress is being made in this direction. But such an integration will not go far toward providing a locus for constructing the necessary situational analyses.

AN ENHANCED PUBLIC ROLE?

The ideal type model for a long-term focused foreign policy advanced in Chapter Three and illustrated in Chapter Four was not designed as an eventual prescriptive model for a future foreign policy bureaucracy. On the contrary, a basic assumption here is that a governmental bureaucracy will not and cannot be expected to make the kind of situational analysis that the model calls for.

The construction of the requisite situational analysis demands a level of objectivity that can be achieved only by an analyst with far more detachment than is to be expected from governmental employees. American foreign policy in an area will be premised necessarily on a set of assumptions. In the case of Iran these assumptions will add up to a conclusion that the Shah can be the cornerstone of a policy designed to help Iran achieve a long-lived stability under a noncommunist regime. In the case of South Vietnam policymakers will support the conclusion that South Vietnam is a victim of aggression and that the National Liberation Front is tightly controlled from Hanoi. Both sets of assumptions may be wrong. But to expect them to be challenged successfully within the bureaucracy in any period short of a severe crisis is to expect too much. Even should one bureaucratic section, such as the Policy Planning Council of the Department of State, achieve the necessary detachment to be able to prepare a situational analysis that runs counter to operating assumptions, it is most unlikely that the vested interests of the foreign policy bureaucracy as a whole would allow for the granting of a fair hearing to a fundamental challenge. A contractual study made outside the bureaucracy by a semiprivate research agency or within a university is even less likely to have an impact since it will lack intrabureaucratic advocates.

The crisis syndrome of diplomacy described in the Introduction may well be in its general outlines an unavoidable manifestation of the type of foreign policy likely to emerge from within the foreign policy bureaucracy. Much can be done to bring a greater range for innovation and to reduce the rigidities of this pattern. The acceptance of a need for diplomatic activity on a covert level as part of a broadly conceived diplomacy and the institutional rationalization of the conduct of this aspect of diplomacy are the kinds of reform that can help bring about these changes. But as soon as the point has been reached at which a policy gives a surface appearance of achieving basic objectives, the situational assumptions on which that policy is based are likely to start becoming rigid. At this point a successful challenge of those assumptions is unlikely within the administration unless the advocates of such a challenge are somehow able to find support within the office of the presidency. Since this latter eventuality can occur only rarely, the conclusion follows that the potential for doing effective long-range planning within the bureaucracy is limited.

This leads to a paradoxical suggestion. Although the increasing complexity of international disputes has given an esoteric quality to diplomacy and has reduced the critical role of the voting public, one part of the answer to the problem of innovative long-term planning may well lie with one section of the attentive public—the academic and nonacademic specialist in the problem area. The non-governmental specialist cannot, of course, escape completely the problem of vested interest that plagues the bureaucrat. He is likely to place a high value on American independence, prestige, and influence and this value in turn will color his view of the world. Furthermore he is unlikely to have been able to maintain as complete a personal detachment in his study of his area of specialty as he might have wished. But compared to the bureaucrat he will appear disinterested. And the personal bias of one specialist is not likely to parallel that of another as will that of bureaucrats with parallel career interests. The primary obstacle preventing the non-governmental area specialist from playing more of a role in long-term planning is not the problem of objectivity but rather the problem of irrelevance.

THE PUBLIC AND THE VIETNAM CRISIS

The Vietnam crisis could provide a fascinating case study of the public role in foreign policy formulation in the atomic era. Public dissatisfaction with administration, diplomatic, and military policy in that area developed rapidly in 1965 and by the summer of 1966 polls indicated a majority of the general public was in one way or another dissatisfied.[11] Within the attentive public the most vociferously expressed dissatisfaction came from those who favored a wide variety of proposals for the de-escalation of the conflict. But the polls had indicated that the majority of those dissatisfied preferred seeing the conflict resolved quickly by a more vigorous use of military force. Thus the most articulate opponents of administration policy were denied any mass base for their opposition and

11. For a summary of the relevant polls and an interpretation see Seymour Martin Lipset, "Doves, Hawks, and Polls," *Encounter*, October 1966, pp. 38–45.

therefore any substantial ability to threaten the administration with defeat at the voting booth.

This disparity in the response of one section of the attentive public and of the general voting public is symptomatic of the altered public role in the age of thermonuclear weaponry. Throughout the mass politics era the general public has tended to see international conflict in simple terms. As Robert Tucker points out in his *The Just War,* the American public in particular, once it is involved in open conflict, quickly adopts a no-holds-barred attitude favoring the successful resolution of the conflict in the shortest time possible and with a minimum loss of American lives.[12] Therefore whereas World War II was easily comprehensible the Korean conflict and even more the Vietnamese conflict are not. American restraint has appeared to many to be damaging to nationalistic self-esteem and a generally bewildering response to what was officially described as unprovoked aggression. The simple truth of General Douglas MacArthur's exhortation that the object of war is victory was self-evident to much of the public and especially to the less-interested public.

Opposition to the conduct of the Korean War from those sections of the attentive public that expressed great dissatisfaction with the conduct of the Vietnamese war was far less vigorous although there was serious questioning of the wisdom of crossing the 38th parallel. A possible explanation of this different behavior is that, first, the attack on South Korea by North Korea presented a picture of aggression that was sufficiently clear-cut to resemble the well-remembered aggressive acts of fascism. Second, the image of communism as a monolith with both the North Koreans and Chinese taking direction from Stalin was widely held. In contrast the origins of the Vietnamese conflict are unclear; and, in fact, a good case has been made for the contention that Hanoi entered into

---

12. Robert Tucker, *The Just War: A Study in Contemporary American Doctrine* (Baltimore, Md., 1960).

a policy of shooting confrontation with Saigon reluctantly and under pressure from communist and other opposition groups being persecuted by the Diem regime.[13] Also, in the decade between the Korean and the Vietnamese conflict, the image of world communism and especially of the Soviet regime changed drastically for much of the attentive public. The image of a monolithic communism bent on pursuing a course of aggression in the fascist model was replaced by the image of a bitterly divided, polycentric communism with some communist regimes becoming so sluggish in their imperialism as to appear to be status quo. What this amounts to is a radically different assumptional base and one that did not permit those accepting it to support a Korea-type response in Vietnam.

Despite their weakness with the electorate, spokesmen for those elements favoring de-escalation have been able to compel the administration repeatedly to state and defend its assumptions. This has been possible because of support within Congress for their positions. However the congressional reaction is not to be explained as a response to public pressure. A far better explanation is that many senators and representatives share the foreign policy assumptions of the supporters of de-escalation.

The primary weakness of the case of the critics of the administration is its vulnerability to the question, "What is your alternative?" Responses to that question fell into two general categories, which can be thought of as tactical and strategic. In the tactical category are those who accept the general strategic objective of a stable, noncommunist government in South Vietnam, Cambodia, and Thailand. Responses here generally call for a moratorium on bombing of North Vietnam, greater efforts to negotiate, and willingness to negotiate with the National Liberation Front. But in no case is the response developed to the point of offering a unified and integrated tactical alternative to administration policy. The closest approxima-

13. Jean Lacouture, *Vietnam: Between Two Truces,* trans. Konrad Kellen and Joel Carmichael (New York, 1966).

tion to a well-reasoned alternative for some time was the enclave idea advanced by General John Gavin.[14] But even this suggestion was unclear regarding its situational assumptions. Lacking a well-formulated alternative tactical plan, these critics have been on weak ground indeed. The Johnson administration has had no difficulty pointing out that it stopped bombing for a brief period; that it offered to negotiate numerous times; that it made as clear as diplomatic language need be its willingness to include the National Liberation Front in negotiations. The constant rejoinder that the administration has not tried hard enough, therefore, appeared to be little more than pointless exhortation. Senator Fulbright's eight-point alternative, which he advances in *The Arrogance of Power*, does go a long way toward filling this void. General situational assumptions are made explicit and the alternative program is carefully integrated within this situational frame. However, the Fulbright program remains a general one, leaving many tactical questions unanswered.

The strategic category of responses can be broken down into three subcategories. In the first of these are those who had previously agreed that containment of communism in Southeast Asia called for the strategic objective of a stable, noncommunist regime in Saigon but have since concluded that the price of achieving such an objective is too high. The point is that the adverse effects on other strategic objectives, especially that of encouraging the liberalization trend in the Soviet Union and other communist states and eventually China, resulting from such tactics as the bombing of North Vietnam, necessitates a reconsideration of basic strategy. But here again alternatives are vaguely stated. Some mention a Laotian-type settlement for Vietnam, the status quo for Cambodia, and further guarantees for the noncommunist regime of Thailand. But there has been no systematic exposition of a revised strategic

14. James M. Gavin, "Communications on Vietnam," *Harper's Magazine*, February, 1966, p. 16.

and tactical plan based on an explicit set of situational assumptions. A second group, including Walter Lippmann and Hans Morgenthau, argue the Mahanist line that American involvement in Southeast Asia constitutes overcommitment. In their view American policy is a clear violation of the long-standing diplomatic rule that no commitment should be made unless there is the power to support it. This does constitute an alternative strategy and one solidly rooted in prenuclear diplomatic practice. American administrations since that of Harry Truman have implicitly concluded that this Mahanist dictum has to be revised in the era of nuclear weaponry. But direct theoretical issue has not been taken with this school of thought and the basic assumptional difference regarding the meaning of "power" in the nuclear era is left unexplored.

The third group consists of a disparate collection of organizations and individuals each calling for unilateral withdrawal from Vietnam and showing no interest in exploring seriously the contention that this would mean the loss in short order of all Southeast Asia to communism. But despite this agreement on prescription, there is a great assumptional diversity within this category. It includes many who view disengagement and disarmament as the key to conflict resolution. Another important element operates more or less explicitly on an assumptional base similar to Hobson's theory of imperialism.[15] To them American policy is determined by a capitalist establishment which needs to control and exploit the economy of Southeast Asia. Their basic solution to the conflict therefore is nothing less than a fundamental change in political control in the United States.

The oft-repeated contention of President Johnson that his critics have no serious alternative to offer to administration policy has had far less validity for those critics who have consistently opposed the strategic objective of stable, noncommunist regimes on the Chinese littoral than for those who have favored this objective. For the former the alternative is a withdrawal of commitments from South-

15. J. A. Hobson, *Imperialism: A Study* (London, 1902).

east Asia either immediately or as rapidly as the demands of prestige and order permit. But for those who advocate containing China by securing noncommunist regimes but who disagree strongly with administration tactics, Johnson's contention has validity. And included in this latter group are most of the senators and representatives who oppose administration policy. The basic question raised here is whether the kind of tightly constructed alternative policy can reasonably be expected to emerge from the public.

THE ROLE OF THE AREA SPECIALIST

One aspect of the public role in the Vietnam case not yet mentioned is the remarkable phenomenon of the "teach-in," which was so pervasive in American universities in 1965. A careful analysis of what was said on these occasions is unlikely to add to the esteem of many American academic figures. Tightly constructed alternative strategies and tactics did not emerge at these gatherings. Still, however, their importance could easily be underrated. The teach-ins symbolized the willingness of many academics who had been almost proud of their noninvolvement in policy issues in the past to become involved at that point. But their involvement did not go so far as to influence the type of scholarly endeavors they were prepared to pursue.

The suggestion here is that the academic area specialist can play a significant role in the policy formulation process without departing from his scholarly standards and without becoming involved in specific policy recommendations. The role he can play is that of constructing situational analyses that have operational relevance. In all likelihood his scholarly work will have indirect relevance if he is at all concerned with the current political process. But in most cases that relevance will not be apparent to the lay reader. Academic area specialists tend to shun detailed analyses of current foreign policy, and for good reason. Access to official documentation is denied the analyst who is not involved in government-approved or contractual research. Policy, therefore, must be inferred from official statements and overt behavior. And in a period in which propositions not based on "hard" data are in increasing disrepute, inferring policy becomes something of an act of courage.

The ideal type model foreign policy developed in Chapter Three and illustrated in Chapter Four is an example of the type of approach that may have operational relevance and at the same time serve as a frame for analyzing an aspect of current foreign policy. An analysis of American policy in South Vietnam by an area specialist following an approach such as this might well provide the basis for a situational analysis in which real rather than ideal tactical or strategic alternatives could be rooted. As noted above, the absence of a carefully drawn situational analysis is the primary deficiency in the vigorous battle of those opposed to further escalation but who agree with the general strategy of containing Communist China. There is no thought here of suggesting that the area specialist step into the official policy formulation process in the role of long-term planner. On the contrary, even contractual political science research for the government tends to reduce the detachment that is so vital for objectivity in constructing situational analyses. This policy role of the academic area specialist should rather be one aspect of an expanded public role. Specifically he should provide the basis for testing the situational assumptions of the official policy-makers. That testing is unlikely to occur directly as a result of his articles and books having been read by concerned bureaucrats. Vested interest attachment to a set of assumptions would more likely lead to easy dismissal than to a serious reconsideration of assumptions. Rather such testing is far more likely to come as a result of pressure from sections of the attentive public and in particular from the Senate Foreign Relations Committee and the House Foreign Affairs Committee. The staffs of these two committees could play a central part in an expanded role for academics in foreign policy formulation. Far from sharing the vested interests of the bureaucracy, the members of these staffs have vested interests in discovering deficiencies in official policy. They might well be influenced by soundly based situational analyses that in some respects run counter to official assumptions. Such studies should be helpful to the staffs in preparing committee hearings in which official situational assumptions could be explored and in some cases challenged. To the extent that the staffs include men with a broad range of area expertise, this could be done for just about any foreign policy problem area. At the very least the hearings should compel the foreign policy bureaucracy to review and reassess the assumptional base of its policy. Optimum results would be obtained if the hearings compelled administration spokesmen to make situational projections that require a prior identification and investigation of relevant trends.

This suggestion does call for a radical departure in scholarly foreign policy analysis but one which could help reduce the sterility of much present analysis. Nor need a focus on current foreign policy place the academic analyst in direct competition with the journalist. The type of operationally relevant situational analysis proposed here calls for a tightly constructed frame within which attitudinal and perceptual trends can be categorized and evaluated. Identifying and exploring these trends requires the application of sophisticated survey-research techniques. At the very best, however, the situational analysis will consist of no more than an elaborate propositional frame. But herein lies the advantage of current analysis. Projected trend developments based on the situational analysis can be tested against observed trend developments. Where observed behavior diverges sharply from anticipated behavior, a direction for revision and refinement of the frame can be given. Where observed behavior and anticipated behavior coincide, some confirmation will have been granted the propositional frame. In either case the analyst should be able to sharpen considerably his understanding of the impact of foreign policy on a target community.

In the American-Iranian case study, perceived American policy objectives for Iran were accepted and an ideal type strategic and tactical plan devised for their achievement. Where the analyst's purpose is to evaluate and analyze existing policy this procedure must be followed. But the ideal type foreign policy model lends itself as well to an exploration of the practicality of a set of general objectives that the analyst believes may be far more desirable than are official objectives. A development of a strategic and tactical plan for achieving these objectives along the lines of this model should compel the analyst to look at many of the requirements for an effective policy on the operational level. This points to another contribution the academic area specialist could make to an enhanced public role in foreign policy formulation. Whereas the bureaucratic area specialist is, at least in noncrisis periods, unlikely to diverge from official policy objectives in his thinking, the academic is not under equal restraint. He can take sharply different policy objectives and devise and examine strategic and tactical schemes for their achievement. Where a careful examination indicates feasibility for the new objectives others in the attentive public may propose their being substituted for existing policy objectives.

In sum, what is suggested here is that the nongovernmental area expert has a very special role to play in the formulation of foreign policy. He can do this without becoming an adjunct member of the bureaucracy or of sacrificing his scholarly standards. By providing the attentive public and a competing foreign policy elite in the legislative branch with a sound assumptional base for alternative strategies or even alternative general objectives, he can help bring about a re-examination of an administration's foreign policy assumptions. And such periodic re-examinations are necessary to prevent whatever long-term planning may be done from becoming rigid doctrine.

INDEX